Contents

The edition of *King Lear* used in the compilation
of these notes is the Arden Edition, edited by
Kenneth Muir, Methuen, London, 1959.

YORK NOTES

General Editors: Professor A.N. Jeffares (*University of Stirling*) & Professor Suheil Bushrui (*American University of Beirut*)

William Shakespeare

KING LEAR

Notes by Robert M. Rehder

BA MA PH D (PRINCETON)
Senior Lecturer in English Studies, University of Stirling

LONGMAN
YORK PRESS

YORK PRESS
Immeuble Esseily, Place Riad Solh, Beirut

ADDISON WESLEY LONGMAN LIMITED
Edinburgh Gate, Harlow,
Essex CM20 2JE, England
Associated companies, branches and representatives
throughout the world

First published 1980
Twenty-second impression 1997

ISBN 0-582-02277-0

Produced by Longman Singapore Publishers Pte Ltd
Printed in Singapore

Part 1

Introduction

The life of William Shakespeare

William Shakespeare is the greatest English writer and perhaps the greatest writer in any language. The exact date of his birth is not known. He was baptised in Holy Trinity Church in Stratford-upon-Avon on 26 April 1564 and is presumed to have been born in the same month. Stratford was then a small market town full of elms on the north bank of the River Avon in Warwickshire with a population in 1590 of about 1,500.

Shakespeare's grandfather, Richard, was a prosperous tenant farmer who lived in Snitterfield, a village north of Stratford. He died before Shakespeare was born. Shakespeare's father, John, did not follow his father's profession. He moved to Stratford and served a seven-year apprenticeship to become a glover and whittawer (a person who cures soft leathers). He made and sold gloves and a variety of leather goods, was a dealer in wool and barley, and invested in real estate. He bought four houses in Stratford. It is not known when he moved to Stratford, but the family lived for nearly fifty years in the big house in Henley Street in which Shakespeare was born.

John Shakespeare was widely respected in Stratford. Beginning in 1556, he held most of the important offices in the town government, and was elected bailiff (mayor) in 1568 when his son William was four. After 1576 he experienced financial difficulties. He stopped coming to meetings of the town council, exchanged land for cash and was sued for debt, but he appears, nevertheless, to have weathered the storm and to have retained the respect of his neighbours.

Between 1556 and 1558 John Shakespeare married Mary Arden, a member of a very old Warwickshire family. She was the daughter of the rich farmer from whom Richard Shakespeare had rented his land and she inherited most of her father's estate. William Shakespeare was their third child and eldest son. He had seven sisters and brothers: Joan (1558–9 or 1560?), Margaret (1562–3), Gilbert (1566–1612), Joan (1569–1646; as the first Joan died in infancy the parents used the name again, a common practice at that time), Anne (1571–9), Richard (1574–1613) and Edmund (1580–1607).

William outlived all his brothers and sisters except Joan, and only he and Joan married. Gilbert became a haberdasher and is recorded as living in both Stratford and London, Joan married a hatter and stayed in Stratford, but no trace of Richard has been found in the surviving records. Edmund, however, seems to have followed his brother, William, to London. He, too, became an actor and was buried in St Saviour's Cathedral, not far from the Globe Theatre.

John Shakespeare died in 1601, in his early seventies, a ripe old age for the time. He lived to see his son become a famous and successful dramatist and the owner of the second largest house in Stratford. Mary Shakespeare died in 1608.

Shakespeare apparently had an orthodox Protestant upbringing. Although his works suggest that he was a sceptical rather than a religious man, he was, like most Englishmen of his time, a regular church-goer. Church-going on Sundays was required by law. This ordinarily meant attending two services every Sunday, one in the morning and one in the afternoon, and taking Communion at least three times a year. Anyone who did not go to church was liable to be fined. In Stratford all business stopped on Sundays and Holy Days, shops and ale-houses were closed, and all fairs and markets ceased. Shakespeare knew the Bible in the Geneva translation. His plays contain references to eighteen of the thirty-nine books of the Old Testament and to eighteen of the twenty-seven books of the New Testament. He was especially attracted to Genesis, Matthew, Job and Ecclesiastes.

Shakespeare probably attended the King's New School in Stratford. The teachers were unusually well qualified in Shakespeare's time and he received a better than average secondary education. Children started at the petty school at four or five where they learned the alphabet, the catechism, prayers and simple arithmetic, then at six or seven they went to the grammar school where they studied almost nothing but Latin (although part of the Greek New Testament was sometimes read). The principal subject was Latin grammar and they read Terence, Cicero, Virgil, Ovid, Horace, Juvenal, Martial and Seneca. Shakespeare demonstrates some knowledge of all of these authors in his works. Ben Jonson who knew him well said that he had 'small *Latine* and less *Greeke*,' but Jonson seems to have been judging Shakespeare by the standards of his own considerable classical scholarship.

After leaving school, Shakespeare may have worked in his father's leather-goods shop. He married Anne Hathaway, the daughter of a farmer who lived in Shottery, a village near Stratford, in November 1582. Shakespeare was eighteen, she was twenty-six and three months pregnant when they were married. This may have been why they applied for a special licence to be married without having the banns read in church on three successive Sundays as was the more normal practice. They had three children: Susanna (1583–1635) and twins, Hamnet (1585–96) and Judith (1585–1662). Both his daughters married, but Shakespeare lived to know only one of his grandchildren, Susanna's daughter, Elizabeth, born in February 1608. Shakespeare's marriage does not appear to have been especially happy because he lived most of his life in London, while Anne seems to have remained in Stratford, although he did invest much of the money he made in Stratford and did return there at the end of his life.

Nothing is known about Shakespeare's life between 1585 and 1592 except that at some time in those years he established himself as an actor and playwright in London. The best attested story is that Shakespeare was 'a Schoolmaster in the Countrey'—where is not specified. The source of this information is William Beeston whose father had been a member of the same company of actors as Shakespeare in 1598. It is possible that Shakespeare joined one of the London companies when they performed in Stratford, as five companies, including the most important, played in Stratford in 1586-7.

The first document to connect Shakespeare with an acting company is an entry in the Accounts of the Treasurer of the Queen's Chamber dated 15 March 1595 that lists William Kempe, William Shakespeare and Richard Burbage as the three members of the Lord Chamberlain's Company who received the money in payment for plays recently performed before Queen Elizabeth. As Kempe was then the most popular comedian in London and Burbage the company's best actor and major shareholder, this indicates that by 1595 Shakespeare was well established in the company. He remained with the Lord Chamberlain's Company for the rest of his career. He wrote all his plays for it and helped to make it, by the end of Queen Elizabeth's reign, the best theatrical company in Britain. Such was its quality that King James chose to become its patron in 1603. During Shakespeare's lifetime, the company performed at court more often than all its rivals combined. Only three or four of the other companies lasted twenty years, but Shakespeare's company continued for almost fifty years. On his death bed, Shakespeare remembered in his will not only his family but his three principal colleagues in the company.

The English drama was transformed about 1540. A new drama based upon the Italian drama came into being. Eleven of Shakespeare's plays are set in Italy and many more are based upon Italian sources. The first English comedies in five acts are *Ralph Roister Doister* (1553?) and *Gammer Gurton's Needle* (1553 or 1554?). The first English tragedy is *Gorboduc*, performed in 1561-2. Before this tragedies were in Latin. James Burbage caused the first commercial playhouse, The Theatre, to be built in Shoreditch in 1576, and Queen Elizabeth formed her own company of actors in 1583. From this time until 1642, when all the theatres were closed by the puritans, there was at least one good professional company of actors established in London and sometimes many. There were more companies of professional actors in proportion to the population in England during the reigns of Queen Elizabeth and James I than there are now.

The actors' companies were repertory companies with their own stock of plays and sometimes with their own playwrights. They presented a different play every day and as many as ten to fifteen different plays a month: An actor might perform in fifty to sixty plays a year. These companies were composed of sharers, hired men and boys. The sharers were the experienced actors who had put up the capital for the enterprise. They managed the company, supervised the productions (there were no directors in Shakespeare's theatre) and shared in the profits. The hired men were all those who were paid weekly wages by the sharers. They included not only the minor actors, but also the musicians, wardrobe keepers, prompters and others needed to stage the plays. The boys were specially trained young boys whose voices had not yet changed, who played the women's and children's parts. It was unusual for a company to employ more than six boys at any one time, some of whom would be just beginning their training. There were no actresses on the English stage until after the theatres re-opened in 1660. This helps to explain why Shakespeare wrote comparatively few parts for women and why these parts are, on the whole, shorter than the men's parts, and show less character development. Shakespeare's women rarely show maternal love and are usually shown with their fathers rather than their mothers. Thus, he limited the demands made on the boy actors.

The theatres in which Shakespeare's company performed accommodated about 3,000 people. These theatres were hollow polygons. The stage was a platform, approximately 43 feet by 28 feet and about 5 feet 6 inches high, built from one of the inner sides out into the middle of the unroofed centre area. The audience either sat in covered galleries that ran around the inside or stood in the open space around the stage. This meant that the actor at the front of the stage was closer to the audience than in our modern theatres, which made all the action more intimate, but especially the asides and soliloquies. The lower gallery at the back of the stage was enclosed to form the tiring house or dressing rooms. The upper gallery was occasionally used by the actors when the action of the play required it. There was no proscenium arch and curtain, and no scenery. As there was no need to stop to change the scene, there were no intermissions between scenes. The action of the play was continuous. The 3,900 lines of *Hamlet* that take about four hours in a modern theatre could be performed in about three hours.

Shakespeare was more involved in more aspects of the theatre than any other English playwright, and perhaps more than any other great playwright except Molière. He began possibly as a hired man. He was an important member of the Lord Chamberlain's company by 1595 and is listed as a sharer in various documents of 1598–9 when the company decided to build the Globe on the south bank of the Thames. From this time until 1613 Shakespeare was actively involved in the company's business affairs as well as in the writing and performing of plays. Although he probably acted in all the plays in the company's repertory, including his own, he is only known for certain to have acted in two plays by Ben Jonson, the comedy, *Every Man in His Humour*, in 1598, and the tragedy, *Sejanus, His Fall*, in 1603. This is known because Jonson, the only playwright of his time to prepare his plays for publication, published the cast lists. Because Shakespeare's name in both cases appears at the head of these cast lists, with that of Richard Burbage, it is assumed that he acted one of the major parts.

There is no way of discovering when Shakespeare began to write plays and there is some evidence to suggest that the plays that survive may not be all that he wrote; nevertheless, between about 1590 and 1613, he wrote thirty-eight plays, at the rate of more or less two plays a year. On his last play, *The Two Noble Kinsmen*, he worked with John Fletcher, who succeeded him as the principal playwright of the company. There is also another play, *Sir Thomas More*, that survives in manuscript (it was not performed until this century), on which Shakespeare seems to have worked with four other people, but as a rule he did not collaborate with other authors. He wrote two very successful long poems: *Venus and Adonis* (1593) and *The Rape of Lucrece* (1594). The first went through sixteen editions before 1640 and the second, eight editions. His best known works, apart from his plays, are his 154 sonnets. Some of them were written before 1598, but the collection was not published until 1609. Three shorter poems survive, 'The Passionate Pilgrim' (1599), 'The Phoenix and the Turtle' (1601) and 'A Lover's Complaint' (1609; there is some doubt about this attribution).

The dramatists of Shakespeare's time, with the exception of Ben Jonson, generally made no effort to publish their plays. This was because the law did not allow the author any copyright in his work. There was no legal requirement that a publisher should pay or even ask an author's permission to print his work. Consequently, it was difficult for a playwright to earn any money from publishing his plays and, moreover, the acting companies who did buy them did not want them published. They believed that people would be less likely to pay to see plays that could be read in a book, performed in a theatre. As far as is known Shakespeare did not make any arrangements to publish any of his plays. He wrote them only for the stage. He does not appear to have had anything to do with the eighteen that were published individually during his lifetime. Two of Shakespeare's friends and colleagues in the King's company, John Heminges and Henry Condell, were responsible for the publication of the First Folio, the collected edition of thirty-six of Shakespeare's plays (excluding *Pericles* and *The Two Noble Kinsmen*) that appeared after his death in 1623. They were also responsible for the division of the plays into comedies, histories and tragedies.

The following is a list of Shakespeare's plays in the order in which they were composed, in so far as that can be established (following E.K. Chambers, *William Shakespeare,* Oxford University Press, Oxford, 1930), and divided according to type:

histories	comedies	tragedies
2 Henry VI		
3 Henry VI		
1 Henry VI		
Richard III	The Comedy of Errors	
		Titus Andronicus
	The Taming of the Shrew	
	Two Gentlemen of Verona	
	Love's Labours Lost	
		Romeo and Juliet
Richard II		
	A Midsummer Night's Dream	
King John		
	The Merchant of Venice	
1 Henry IV		
2 Henry IV		
	Much Ado About Nothing	
Henry V		
		Julius Caesar
	As You Like It	
	Twelfth Night	
		Hamlet
	The Merry Wives of Windsor	
		Troilus and Cressida
	All's Well That Ends Well	
	Measure for Measure	
		Othello
		King Lear
		Macbeth
		Antony and Cleopatra
		Coriolanus
		Timon of Athens
		Pericles
		Cymbeline
	The Winters Tale	
	The Tempest	
Henry VIII		
	Two Noble Kinsmen	

This series of works shows that Shakespeare was always ready to come to grips with new material. His beginning with three history plays is especially remarkable. These very successful plays were the first of their kind. There is, as F.P. Wilson states, 'no certain evidence that any popular dramatist before Shakespeare wrote a play based on English history.'* Shakespeare was the only contemporary playwright to make extensive use of historical chronicles. He, moreover, did not simply write on isolated historical subjects, but composed connected groups of plays. He appreciated history as a sequence of events. He was interested in the problems of succession and of development. Others had written plays based on Roman history, but Shakespeare turned to Roman history only after he had explored the history of his own country, and his interest in history does not show only in the history plays. He used historical chronicles to great effect in some of the tragedies.

The above list also shows that after his first successes, Shakespeare immediately tried comedy and then tragedy, and then worked at the various forms alternately, until, after writing *Measure for Measure*, he wrote five of his greatest tragedies one after another, and eight tragedies in a row. Perhaps it was *Hamlet*, apparently composed about a year or so before the death of Shakespeare's father and the first of the great tragedies, that prepares the way for those that follow. Certainly the comedies that he wrote after *Hamlet* are different from those that he had written before. After *Hamlet*, he wrote *The Merry Wives of Windsor*, his only play set in contemporary Britain, and a number of plays in which he combined comedy and tragedy, and in which he considered the nature of fantasy. Shakespeare experimented as long as he continued to write.

Shakespeare's works were very successful and his company prospered. He earned, as a result, a substantial amount of money, much of which he appears to have invested in and around Stratford, which suggests that he always considered Stratford his home. In 1597 he bought New Place, the second largest house there, and, although it had ample grounds, he soon bought some of the adjacent land so as to expand his garden. He inherited his father's house in Henley Street. He bought 127 acres of farmland outside Stratford, and another garden with a cottage in the town in 1602. His largest investment was in 1605 when he bought a half share of the tithes of Old Stratford, Welcombe and Bishopton, three hamlets near Stratford. This meant that the tenants who farmed the land which was included in the tithes made a yearly payment of rent to Shakespeare. He also bought a house in London in 1613. Everything indicates that Shakespeare was a good businessman. His purpose seems to have been not only to provide an income and security for his old age, but also to try to establish himself, his children and grandchildren as gentry in Stratford.

Marlowe and the Early Shakespeare, Oxford University Press, Oxford, 1953.

Shakespeare's works provide the fullest description of his character. There is not very much other information, but the meagre records that do survive suggest that he was a kind man with good manners. Henry Chettle, a London publisher, praises Shakespeare's civil demeanour and 'his uprightness of dealing' in 1592. Anthony Scoloker writes of 'Friendly Shakespeare's Tragedies,' and John Davies describes him in 1603:

> *And though the* stage *doth staine pure, gentle* bloud,
> *Yet generous yee are in* minde *and* moode.

William Barksted, who wrote plays for a rival company, mentions Shakespeare as 'so deere lov'd a neighbor' in 1607. Ben Jonson refers to him as 'My gentle *Shakespeare*' in his poem in the First Folio. Heminges and Condell offer their book 'only to keepe the memory of so worthy a Friend & Fellow aliue, as was our *Shakespeare*,' and speak of him as 'a most gentle expresser' of nature.

William Shakespeare died at the age of 52 and was buried on 23 April 1616 in the church in which he was christened, Holy Trinity Church, Stratford.

A note on the text

The best text of *King Lear* is that of the First Folio (1623). The play was published twice during the author's lifetime, although Shakespeare had nothing to do with either publication. The first quarto appeared in 1608 and the second in 1619 (although it was fraudulently dated 1608). There is a variety of differences between the twelve surviving copies of the first quarto. The second quarto was set up from a copy of the first containing a number of uncorrected sheets. The Folio text seems to have been prepared from a manuscript (perhaps that of a prompt book) and a copy of the first quarto. According to Chambers, the quartos 'omit about 100 lines' found in the Folio and the Folio 'omits about 300 lines' found in the quartos, including all of Act IV Scene 3. Therefore it is necessary for a good edition of the play to compare the surviving copies of the quartos with those of the Folio.

A facsimile of both quartos was published by C. Praetorius, Praetorius, London, 1885. The best facsimile of the First Folio is the one edited by Charlton Hinman, Oxford University Press, New York, 1968.

Anyone wishing an introduction to the very complicated world of Shakespearean textual scholarship should read: A.W. Pollard's *Shakespeare's Fight with the Pirates*, Cambridge University Press, Cambridge, 1920, 1967; W.W. Greg, *The Editorial Problem in Shakespeare*, Oxford University Press, Oxford, third edition, 1954, and F. Bowers, *On Editing Shakespeare*, University Press of Virginia, Charlottesville, 1966.

Part 2

Summaries

of KING LEAR

General summary

Lear, the King of Britain, decides to divide his kingdom among his three daughters. He is an old man who during the last years of his life wants to enjoy being king without assuming the responsibilities of kingship. When he asks his daughters to tell him how much they love him, his favourite daughter, Cordelia, refuses to say anything. He becomes angry, disinherits her and divides the kingdom between her two sisters. The sisters then turn against Lear. When they reject him, Lear goes mad. The country is in disorder. Cordelia, who has married the King of France, returns with an army to aid her father. Through his madness King Lear comes to know himself better. The two sisters defeat Cordelia and Lear, but lose their victory when they fight each other. Cordelia, however, is killed soon after her reconciliation with her father. Lear dies of a broken heart. Self-knowledge has come too late.

Detailed summaries

Act I, Scene 1

The play opens on an empty stage. Three men enter: the Earl of Kent, the Earl of Gloucester and his illegitimate son, Edmund. Kent and Gloucester wonder how the King is going to divide the kingdom. Exactly what is going on is not made clear. Shakespeare often begins his plays in the middle of a conversation or an action.

Kent asks Gloucester if Edmund is his son. Gloucester replies that he used to blush to acknowledge him, but that now he does it without embarrassment. He explains in a somewhat offhand way that Edmund is illegitimate and that, although he has a legitimate son, he does not love Edmund any less. He remembers that his mother was 'fair' and that 'there was good sport at his making'. Thus the subject of parenthood is introduced into the play. Presumably Edmund is standing to one side and does not hear all of this conversation.

Then King Lear enters with his three daughters, Goneril, Regan and Cordelia, and his court. Goneril is married to the Duke of Albany and Regan to the Duke of Cornwall. The two husbands are with their wives. The King asks for a map in order to show those present how he proposes to divide his kingdom. He states that because he is growing old and wishes to approach death without any worries, he is going to give all the 'cares and business' of government to his daughters and their husbands. As his youngest daughter, Cordelia, is about to accept either the King of France or the Duke of Burgundy as her husband, he will divide the kingdom into three parts and give each daughter a share as a dowry. This is the decision that sets all the events in the play in motion.

King Lear asks each of his daughters to speak in turn and says that he will give the largest share to the one who says that she loves him the most (although from what Kent and Gloucester have said it appears that he had already divided everything into three equal portions).

Goneril, the eldest daughter, speaks first, then Regan. They both make elaborate and insincere declarations of their love for their father. After each speech the King shows the speaker her share of the kingdom on his map. As she listens to her sisters, Cordelia thinks out loud that her love cannot be expressed in words. When her turn comes, she states that she has nothing to say. The King replies: 'Nothing will come of nothing: speak again'. She refuses. Again he threatens her and tries several times to persuade her to say how much she loves him. Cordelia stubbornly refuses to say any more than that she loves him as she ought to love her father. This is not enough for Lear. He loses his temper. He swears that she will have neither a share of the kingdom nor any dowry of any kind, and he disclaims her as a daughter. From now on, he says, she will be a stranger to his heart. This is the first of King Lear's many rages.

The Earl of Kent tries to intervene in Cordelia's favour. Lear brushes aside his objections. He declares that Cordelia's share will be divided between her two sisters and their husbands and that they have to share the government of the kingdom jointly. He will keep only a hundred knights and 'the name' of King; all the power and the responsibility will pass to them. Henceforth he will stay alternately for a month at a time with Goneril and Regan.

Kent declares that Lear is mad (I.1.144). This is the first suggestion of Lear's madness. Kent urges Lear to check his 'hideous rashness' and attempts to tell him the truth. He intimates that his youngest daughter is more sincere than her sisters. Lear orders him out of his sight. Kent is as stubborn as Cordelia. He insists that Lear is making a serious mistake. Shakespeare's conception of the tragedy and of Lear's character depends upon Lear being warned that he is behaving wrongly. King Lear chooses his troubles. Shakespeare makes him responsible for his actions. Kent and Lear are both angry. Lear suddenly banishes him. He says that if in ten days Kent is found in the kingdom he will be killed.

Gloucester returns with the King of France and the Duke of Burgundy. Lear informs them that now Cordelia has no dowry and that they may take her or leave her. Burgundy withdraws his offer of marriage. France asks Lear why he has renounced the daughter who a moment before was his favourite. He states that he loves her the more for being rejected and takes her as his Queen.

Cordelia says goodbye to her sisters. 'I know you what you are,' she tells them and directs them to 'Love well our father'. Regan says that Cordelia ought not to speak to them about their duty and Goneril says that she deserves what has happened to her. The scene ends with Regan and Goneril talking among themselves. They observe that their father has shown poor judgement and that he may become increasingly hot-tempered and difficult. They agree to work together.

NOTES AND GLOSSARY

moiety:	share
Liege:	lord
champains:	open country
meads:	meadows
validity:	value
Hecate:	goddess of the underworld
propinquity:	kinship
messes:	portions of food
addition:	titles, ceremonies
reverb:	reverberate
recreant:	traitor
benison:	blessing
loth:	reluctant
plighted:	folded, dissembling

Act I, Scene 2

The first scene has been about Lear and his daughters. The second is about Gloucester and his sons.

Edmund is alone. He is full of resentment about his circumstances. He asserts that even though he is a bastard he is as good as his brother, if not better. Bastards are born 'in the lusty stealth of nature', therefore they represent a more complete human mixture and are more energetic than legitimate children. He declares he must have his brother Edgar's land. He is working himself up to the point of action and waves a letter that he says will help him to overthrow his brother. His father, Gloucester, sees the letter as he enters and asks him what it is. Edmund thrusts it into his pocket and pretends that it is nothing. Gloucester insists on seeing it. Edmund, with assumed reluctance, gives him the letter, saying that it is from his brother, Edgar. The letter, which Edmund has forged, complains that the young do not inherit their fortunes until they are too old to enjoy them and that they suffer 'the oppression of aged tyranny'. It invites Edmund to come and discuss this and promises him half of their father's income if he should happen to die.

Gloucester knows his two sons so little that he accepts the letter as genuine. He cross-examines Edmund about what Edgar has said to him recently. Like Lear he is moved to anger and calls Edgar an 'Unnatural, detested brutish villain'. Edmund suggests that he speak to Edgar to discover if there has been a misunderstanding and that Gloucester should hide where he can overhear the conversation. Gloucester agrees. He is deeply disturbed that the son whom he loves so much might not return his love. Thinking of Lear's unnatural behaviour to Cordelia and Kent, which he has just witnessed, and of his own troubles, he feels that the order of the world is crumbling. He attributes all this to the recent eclipses of the sun and moon. He imagines a future full of discord and treachery.

After Gloucester has left, Edmund mocks his belief in the powers of the stars. Men, he says, refuse to assume the responsibility for their evil actions. They blame them on supernatural powers. He would have been what he is whatever star shone on the night of his conception. Edgar enters. Edmund pretends to be seriously concerned about Gloucester's anger against Edgar. He tells Edgar that he has offended their father so much that Gloucester might attack him, and persuades Edgar to come to his rooms so that he can explain matters and to come armed.

NOTES AND GLOSSARY

curiosity:	fastidiousness
fops:	fools
sirrah:	sir, an ordinary form of address to inferiors
auricular:	spoken (literally: heard)
bias:	shape of a bowl which causes it to roll in a predictable curve
spherical predominance:	predominance of a particular planet in a horoscope
Ursa major:	constellation of the Great Bear
Tom o' Bedlam:	madman (Bedlam: the hospital of St Mary of Bethlehem in London for the mentally ill)
sectary:	believer

Act I, Scene 3

The scene shifts to the residence of the Duke of Albany. Goneril is complaining to her steward, Oswald, about the erratic and riotous behaviour of her father and his men. She informs Oswald that she will not speak to King Lear when he returns from hunting. She orders Oswald to be negligent and cold in serving Lear and his knights. She describes the King as an old fool who desires to exercise the authority he has given away. He is a child who must be managed like a child. She wants, she says, to create more trouble.

NOTES AND GLOSSARY
chiding: scolding
upbraid: censure
check: rebuke

Act I, Scene 4

Kent appears in disguise. He is determined to try to help Lear. When Lear and his men return from the hunt, Kent asks the King if he can enter his service. Lear accepts him and calls for his dinner and his Fool. There is no one to receive them. Oswald walks in and out without paying any attention to Lear. King Lear and one of his knights discuss the fact that Goneril's servants have become unkind and unwilling to serve them. Oswald re-enters. Lear asks him: 'Who am I, sir?' He answers not 'the King' but: 'My Lady's father', emphasising Lear's dependence on his daughters. Lear swears at Oswald and Kent trips him.

The Fool enters. He applauds Kent 'for taking one's part that's out of favour', meaning Lear, but says that if Kent continues he will need his coxcomb, the cap of the professional fool. The Fool makes a series of jokes and songs about Lear being a fool for having given away his kingdom.

Goneril appears and rebukes the King for the insolence, carping and quarrelling of his men. Lear is shocked by her addressing him in this way. He asks: 'Are you our daughter?' and 'Who is it that can tell me who I am?' This is the same question he has already put to Oswald. It appears that in giving away his kingdom he has sacrificed his identity. Goneril states that his men have made her palace like a tavern or brothel and that either he must reduce their number or she will do it. Lear calls her a 'Degenerate bastard'. He says he has another daughter left and orders his horses saddled. Albany arrives on the scene as Lear is raging at Goneril. He protests that he is ignorant of what is going on.

Lear sees that in wronging Cordelia over a trifle he has upset the order of things. He strikes his head and cries 'O Lear, Lear, Lear! / Beat at this gate, that let thy folly in, / And thy dear judgment out!' He calls on Nature to dry up Goneril's womb and to make her sterile, or, if she has a child, to make it without affection for her so that she feels what it is like to have a thankless child. This, one of the most terrible curses a father could pronounce on a daughter, shows how deeply Lear is affected by Goneril's behaviour and how great is his need of gratitude. This is the same need that caused him to want Cordelia to say how much she loved him. Before he leaves, Lear is crying. He declares to Goneril that he is 'asham'd / That thou hast power to shake my manhood thus,' but that he will go to his other daughter. She (not Lear himself) will revenge him and 'Thou shalt find / That I'll resume the shape which thou dost think / I have cast off for ever.'

After King Lear and his men have left, Albany tries to tell Goneril that she may have gone too far. She pays little attention to him. She is intent on reducing the number of Lear's knights so that he is no way a threat to her. She despatches Oswald to Regan with a letter explaining what she has done and asking for her sister's support.

NOTES AND GLOSSARY

defuse:	disguise
roundest:	plainest
lubber:	lout
coxcomb:	cap of professional fool
Nuncle:	uncle
brach:	hound bitch
trowest:	suppose
motley:	parti-coloured clothing of professional fool
frontlet:	headband
peascod:	peapod
rank:	gross, coarse
weal:	commonwealth
fraught:	loaded
debosh'd:	debauched
epicurism:	luxury
disquantity:	make smaller
besort:	suit
cadent:	falling
untented:	uncleaned

Act I, Scene 5

Lear sends Kent with a letter to Regan, presumably informing her of his coming. The Fool says to the King that his other daughter will be like this one just as two sour crab apples taste alike. If the King were a Fool, he continues, he would beat him for being old before his time. He has become old without becoming wise. Lear is aware of the turmoil in his mind. He replies: 'O! let me not be mad, not mad, sweet heaven; / Keep me in temper; I would not be mad!'

Thus Shakespeare increases our expectation and prepares us for what is to happen.

NOTES AND GLOSSARY
kibes: chilblains
mo: more

Act II, Scene 1

On his way to meet Edgar, Edmund is told that the Duke and Duchess of Cornwall are to visit the Earl of Gloucester and that there are rumours of war between the Dukes of Cornwall and Albany. When Edmund meets his brother he says that their father is watching his rooms and that Edgar must save himself at once. He tells Edgar that the Duke of Cornwall is coming and questions him as to whether he has spoken against Cornwall. Edgar states that he has not said a word. Then Edmund draws his sword. He persuades Edgar to engage him in a brief mock combat and then to escape. As Edgar runs away, Edmund wounds himself with his own sword, cries for his brother to stop and calls to his father for help.

Gloucester rushes in. Edmund relates that Edgar tried to persuade him to murder Gloucester and that when he expressed his horror of parricide Edgar wounded him with his sword. He states that when he fought back Edgar fled. Gloucester believes him. He intends to arrange with the Duke of Cornwall to have Edgar hunted down, tried and executed. Preparing himself for the possibility of Edgar's capture, Edmund maintains that Edgar told him that because he was a bastard no one would accept his word against that of the legitimate son, saying that if Edmund revealed his plan, he would simply deny the truth of everything Edmund said. Gloucester praises Edmund for his loyalty. He says that he will arrange for him to inherit his land.

Trumpets sound announcing the arrival of Cornwall and Regan. They have heard the story of Edgar. They express surprise. Gloucester declares to Regan: 'O Madam, my old heart is crack'd, it's crack'd'. Regan makes it out that Edgar's behaviour is the result of his being with Lear's 'riotous knights'. Her sister has written to inform her of her difficulties with them and to warn her not to be at home if Lear comes to stay with her. This is why she and Cornwall have come to visit Gloucester. Cornwall praises Edmund for doing his duty to his father. He says he needs men he can trust and asks Edmund to enter his service.

NOTES AND GLOSSARY

bussing:	kissing
toward:	impending
fell:	fierce
gasted:	aghast, terrified
fast'ned:	hardened, confirmed
capable:	able to inherit
bewray:	reveal

Act II, Scene 2

Kent encounters Oswald before Gloucester's castle. He picks a quarrel with him, abusing him with a long list of bad names. Kent's speeches are a good example of Shakespeare's extraordinary power of invective. He often uses this power for the purposes of comedy. This scene, like the scenes with the Fool, provides some relief from the mounting tension of the tragedy. At the same time Kent's purpose is serious and the scene demonstrates the aggressive passions with which the play is concerned. Oswald is dumbfounded because he believes they have never met. Kent reminds him that he tripped him two days ago. He draws his sword and challenges Oswald. All Oswald does is cry for help. Kent beats him until Cornwall, Regan, Gloucester and Edmund intervene to rescue him.

Cornwall tries to discover the cause of the dispute. Kent continues to abuse Oswald who pretends that he did not fight because of Kent's age. Kent is carried away by his anger. He insults Cornwall who orders him put in the stocks. Kent protests that he serves the King. For Regan and Cornwall this is another reason for punishing him. Gloucester protests that this will offend the King. He is overruled.

NOTES AND GLOSSARY

broken meats:	remains of someone else's food
super-serviceable:	above one's work
one-trunk-inheriting:	poor, owning only one trunkful of belongings
thy addition:	this list of names that I have given you
I'll make a sop o' th' moonshine of you:	I will pierce so many holes in you that you will soak up the moonlight
cullionly:	basely
barber-monger:	one who is always going to the barber
carbonado:	to score a piece of meat before grilling it
unbolted:	unsifted, coarse
jakes:	privy
intrince:	intricate
smoile:	smile

Fortune's wheel: Fate is personified as a goddess who turns a wheel which represents the changes that occur in life. The sense here is that one moment a person can be at the bottom, the next, at the top (compare V.3.174).

Act II, Scene 3

Edgar is alone on the stage. He describes how he heard himself proclaimed a wanted man and hid in a hollow tree from the hunt. Now there is no safe place for him in the kingdom. A watch is kept for him everywhere. He decides, like Kent, to disguise himself. He will make himself appear the poorest, basest, most miserable and insignificant man possible. He smears himself with dirt, tangles his hair and strips himself naked except for a blanket so as to resemble one of the mad beggars that wander about the country. He practices the whining speech of these beggars: 'Poor Turlygood! poor Tom!' and declares that nothing remains of his former self.

NOTES AND GLOSSARY
elf: tangle
presented: exposed

Act II, Scene 4

King Lear, the Fool and the King's men enter to find Kent in the stocks. Lear will not believe that Cornwall and Regan have imprisoned his messenger. Every time that Kent says 'yes' Lear says 'no'. With Kent before him in the stocks, obviously knowing better than anyone how he got there, this is a perfect example of Lear's refusal to accept reality. Similarly, at the beginning of the play, he does not want to see his daughters as they are. After Kent relates in detail how he came to be put in the stocks, Lear cries out:

O! how this mother swells up towards my heart;
Hysterica passio! down, thou climbing sorrow!
Thy element's below. Where is this daughter?
(II.4.56–8)

The *mother* or *hysterica passio* are old names for a disease that choked or suffocated women and was thought to come from the womb. Here and elsewhere in the play Lear seems to feel that he is both father and mother to his daughters. He relives their lives in a sense, thinking of their conception and birth, and of himself feeding them. He feels they are a part of him and identifies himself with them. When they turn against him, he is as if attacked by parts of himself. This speech also shows that he is being overwhelmed from the inside. Hysteria, passion, sorrow well up within. They come from below and move toward his heart. Thus Lear's madness appears as a defence against subterranean or unconscious emotion, against what he cannot bear to feel.

As if afraid of what he will discover, he instructs Kent and the Fool to wait for him, while he goes to look for his daughter. Kent asks why the King has so few men with him. The Fool, who prefers never to answer any question directly, answers him with a series of epigrams and a rhyme. The men have left because they have seen that the King's fortunes are declining. Men who serve for gain pack when it begins to rain and leave you in the storm. Because he is a Fool, he will remain loyal to the King. His word-play disguises his real affection for Lear.

King Lear returns, having been told that Cornwall and Regan are too tired to see him. He vacillates between anger and trying to persuade himself that it may be true. Then he looks again at Kent in the stocks and decides that he will speak to them now even if it means that he has to beat a drum outside their door in order to wake them up. He sends Gloucester to fetch them and says, half to himself: 'O me! my heart, my rising heart! but, down!'

Gloucester returns with Cornwall and Regan. Lear starts to explain his deeply felt grievance against Goneril. Her unkindness is a vulture eating his heart. Regan brings him up sharply by saying that she hopes that he undervalues what is due to Goneril rather than that she has come short of her duty. She declares that she cannot believe that her sister would not do her duty. If she has restrained Lear's men it is for good reasons and for a good purpose. She tells her father that he is old and at the end of his life. He should allow himself to be ruled by those who know what is right for him better than he does himself. Return to Goneril, she urges, and apologise. Lear mocks the idea: should a father ask his daughter to forgive him for being old? Again Regan urges him to return to her sister.

King Lear begins to curse Goneril. He calls down 'all the stor'd vengeances of Heaven' upon her. When Regan says that he will curse her in the same way 'when the rash mood is on', he tells her that she will never treat him as her sister has done. This is an appeal for her love. Lear pleads for her kindness. If he could, he would compel her to love him, but instead he names all the things that he can think of that ought to make her be kind to him: 'The offices of nature, bond of childhood, / Effects of courtesy, dues of gratitude'. He then reminds her that he has given her half the kingdom. This shows his doubts that her love will be offered spontaneously.

Just as Lear is demanding who put Kent in the stocks, a trumpet sounds. Oswald enters followed by Goneril. Lear asks the Heavens to help him: 'if you yourselves are old . . . send down and take my part!', a sign that he does not feel he can rely upon himself and that he feels his daughters are too strong for him. He persists in wanting to know who put Kent in the stocks. Cornwall admits that he did and states that Kent deserved worse. Regan tells him that if he will return to Goneril now and dismiss half his men, he can come to her at the end of the month with the remaining fifty. Lear objects. The images he uses foreshadow what is to come. He states he would rather give up all roofs and 'be a comrade with the wolf and owl' than return with Goneril. Goneril says that the choice is his. Lear replies: 'do not make me mad' and calls her a disease of his flesh. He will not scold her. She can repent of her behaviour at her leisure. He and all his hundred men can stay with Regan.

Regan demurs. She has not expected him to come at this time. She does not have enough provisions. Yet again she urges him to return with Goneril. Lear will not. Regan and Goneril both reproach him for having so many men, then Regan adds that if he comes he can bring no more than twenty-five men. Lear does not want to believe what he hears. He sees that he is caught between the two women. Goneril, he says, is not the worst. Fifty is better than twenty-five. He will return with her. Goneril asks him why he needs twenty-five men. Ten or five are enough in her house where there are so many servants to wait on him.

Lear is at his wits' end. It is not a question of need. If man has only what he needs he is an animal. Even the poorest beggar has something more than he needs merely to exist. A woman chooses her clothes in order to be beautiful, not simply to be warm, he says, looking at his daughters' clothes. He is about to explain 'true need' when he breaks off, overcome by the conflicting emotions of anger and sorrow. Unable to construct any argument, he confesses his misery:

> You see me here, you Gods, a poor old man,
> As full of grief as age; wretched in both!

Lear's many invocations of the gods are the sign of his own helplessness. Forsaken by his daughters and those around him, he speaks instead to the heavens. This represents a withdrawal from the world. Having surrendered his own power, he retains only the habit of command. Unable to control the world, he commands the heavens to control it for him. He asks the gods to make him angry and to prevent him from crying. This speech shows us the break-up of his mind. His wishes become increasingly confused, his statements contradictory. He tells his daughters that he will be revenged on them, but as yet he does not know how. Whatever he does, it will be terrible. He insists that despite all the reasons he has to weep, that he will not weep. My heart, he cries out, will break into a hundred thousand fragments before I will weep.

This makes it appear that he loses his sanity because of his inability to accept the profound sadness that he feels. His last words before leaving the stage are: 'O Fool! I shall go mad'. Gloucester, Kent and the Fool leave with him.

Cornwall observes that a storm is coming. Regan almost shows some pity for Lear when she remarks that Gloucester's house is too small for him to be comfortably lodged, but she refers to him as 'the old man', not as her father. Goneril states that it is his own fault and they both agree that they would be glad to receive him alone, but without a single follower. Gloucester re-enters to report that King Lear is outside 'in high rage', calling for a horse and about to go out into the night and the storm. The wind, he says, is blowing hard and for miles around the house there is only an occasional bush for shelter. Goneril tells Gloucester not to try to persuade Lear to stay. Regan and Cornwall order him to close his doors and leave Lear to the storm.

NOTES AND GLOSSARY

spite of intermission: in spite of delay

meiny:	servants
fetches:	tricks
remotion:	keeping aloof
buttered his hay:	Dishonest ostlers put grease on the hay of horses entrusted to them so that the horses would not eat the hay and that they would be able to keep the money that otherwise they would have had to spend on feed.
sumpter:	pack-horse, drudge
flaws:	fragments

Act III, Scene 1

Kent encounters one of King Lear's gentlemen. They are searching for the King in the stormy night. The characters make many references to the weather and to the landscape because this is the only way that Shakespeare can present them to the audience (see p.8). The gentleman has been with Lear. He describes him as out of his mind, wandering about in the wind and rain, shouting at the elements to destroy the world and tearing his white hair. He compares the storm inside Lear's mind with the storm outside. The King, he says, 'Strives in his little world of man to out-storm / The to-and-fro-conflicting wind and rain'. Lear is being driven in all directions by his 'to-and-fro-conflicting' emotions. The gentleman tells Kent that only the Fool is with Lear, trying to help him laugh away his pain.

Kent, who recognises the gentleman and knows that he is a man he can trust, confides to him that there is trouble coming between the Dukes of Albany and Cornwall, and that a French army has landed on the south coast. He tells the gentleman that he is more than he seems and sends him to tell Cordelia, who is with the French at Dover, what has happened to the King. He gives him a purse and his ring so that Cordelia will know from whom the message comes.

NOTES AND GLOSSARY

snuffs: resentments
packings: plots

Act III, Scene 2

King Lear and the Fool are together. Lear shouts at the winds to rage and blow. He commands the storm not only to destroy the world, but also to break the moulds and the germens or seeds that Nature uses to create men, because men are ungrateful. He is thinking of his daughters and wants to abolish even the possibility of their existence. The Fool tries to persuade him to go back to the house. Kent finds them. He declares that he cannot remember a worse storm with such lightning and thunder.

Lear does not recognise Kent. He tells him to tremble because he contains 'undivulged crimes' unpunished by Justice and 'close pent-up guilts'. Hidden crimes will be found out and punished. This is the first reference to justice in the play. Lear is talking to Kent but thinking about his own troubles. Perhaps it could be said that he goes mad as a defence against his own guilty feelings. The speeches that Lear makes in his madness are usually about himself and his daughters. They are not incoherent ravings and all of them make some kind of sense. Kent says that there is a hut nearby, and persuades Lear to take shelter there. Lear admits that he is cold. He is also concerned about the Fool. He does not want him to suffer. He follows Kent off the stage, leaving the Fool to make the final speech in the scene. The Fool speaks in paradoxes. He prophesies that when certain things happen, Albion (an old name for Britain) will come to such 'great confusion' that people will use their feet for walking. Some of the things he mentions ('When brewers mar their malt with water') are already happening and others ('When every case in law is right') will never happen. He marks the difference between the real and the ideal world, and the topsy-turvy nature of reality. As people already use their feet for walking, his conclusion suggests that the world is not going to change.

NOTES AND GLOSSARY

thought-executing: acting with the speed of thought
vaunt-couriers: heralds

court holy-water:	flattery
pudder:	turmoil
summoner:	official who ordered offenders before an ecclesiastical court

Act III, Scene 3

The scene shifts back to Gloucester's house. Gloucester tells Edmund that he is unhappy about the 'unnatural' way in which Lear has been treated, and although Goneril, Regan and Cornwall have forbidden him on pain of death to help the King in any way, he will look after him secretly. The injuries done to King Lear will soon be revenged. The Dukes of Albany and Cornwall are no longer on good terms, and this night he has received a letter saying that there is an army now marching to the King's aid. He directs Edmund to say nothing about all of this. He asks him to engage Cornwall in conversation so that Cornwall does not find out what he is doing. As soon as he leaves, Edmund declares that he will instantly tell the Duke everything his father has said. Everything that his father loses, he will gain. 'The younger rises when the old doth fall.'

Act III, Scene 4

Kent, Lear and the Fool have found the hut. Kent invites Lear to go inside. Lear refuses. The storm is nothing beside 'This tempest in my mind'. All he feels is the ingratitude of his children to whom he has given everything. Again he is divided between thoughts of punishing Regan and Goneril and of weeping over them, but he punishes himself by staying out in the storm. Kent urges him to go in. He agrees, but insists that the Fool go in first. He calls him 'boy' and thinks of him as if he were another child. Lear muses on all the poor who have no houses. He has thought too little about the poor, he says. If the rich would expose themselves to what the poor feel, they might give what they do not need to the poor, and the world would be more just.

A voice speaks from within the hut. The Fool rushes out crying for help and saying there is a spirit inside. Edgar emerges disguised as poor Tom, the mad beggar. Smeared with dirt and wearing only a blanket, he confronts the dishevelled and rain-soaked Lear. Thus Shakespeare brings the man who is pretending to be mad face to face with the man who is mad. For Lear it is as if he is looking in a mirror. He sees himself in Edgar. His first question to him is: 'Didst thou give all to thy daughters?'

Edgar's statements are deliberately disconnected and interspersed with rhymes and snatches of song. He talks about being pursued by the devil or foul fiend who tempts him to suicide, and keeps repeating that he is cold. Lear laments that Edgar's unkind daughters have left him in this state. He inquires what he was. Edgar replies that he was a servingman who wore elegant clothes, drank, gambled and chased after women. He warns Lear against lust. Lear responds that Edgar would be better dead than to suffer this weather without any clothes. A man does not grow his own coat as animals do. He looks at his companions, Kent and the Fool, and remarks that the three of them in their clothes are 'sophisticated', but that Edgar, naked except for his blanket, is 'unaccommodated man'. He shows what man really is: 'a poor, bare, forked animal'. Lear tries to take off his clothes so that he will be as he imagines Edgar to be, reduced to his essential humanity. This is an attempt at honesty. He wants to strip himself of everything false and alien. He refers to his clothes as 'lendings,' as if they were not his and he had only borrowed them. He seeks to uncover his true self. The Fool dissuades him by saying that it is a wicked night in which to go swimming.

The conversation is interrupted by the appearance of Gloucester with a torch. Edgar, who is afraid his father will recognise him, calls him a devil. He exaggerates his act as a madman. Gloucester wants Lear to come to his house. His daughters, he tells him, hope that he will die if he is left without shelter or food in the cold and wet. He commiserates with Lear, saying that he is almost mad himself. He has a son whom he loved more than anything, but who is outlawed because he tried to kill his father. Thus Edgar begins to hear the truth about what has happened to him. Lear wants to stay and talk to Edgar, to whom he keeps referring as a learned man and 'my philosopher', rather than go with Gloucester. Kent suggests to Gloucester that they take Edgar with them as his presence seems to make Lear happy and they go off together.

NOTES AND GLOSSARY

superflux:	superfluity
pelican daughters:	the mother pelican was thought to pierce her breast with her bill and thus feed her young with her own blood
Pillicock:	term of endearment, darling (here suggested by *pelican*)
plackets:	opening in a petticoat
cat:	civet cat
lendings:	borrowed things
aroint:	be gone
sallets:	salads, something tasty
tithing:	a district containing ten families

Act III, Scene 5

Edmund is alone with Cornwall. He has obviously just told him Gloucester's secret news as Cornwall's first words are: 'I will have my revenge ere I depart his house'. Edmund hands him the letter informing Gloucester of the army on its way to aid the King. He says that he wishes he had not been the one to discover this treason. Cornwall praises his loyalty and states that now he is the Earl of Gloucester. He asks him to come with him to tell Regan and then to go and look for his father. Edmund says as an aside that he hopes he finds Gloucester comforting the King as that will make things worse for his father. To Cornwall, he promises that he will be loyal despite the conflict between that loyalty and his natural feelings as a son.

Act III, Scene 6

Once inside Lear decides to bring his daughters to trial. He forsakes the idea of revenge for the regular processes of justice. Amid the chaos of his madness he has a desire for order. He orders Edgar and the Fool to sit with him and be the judges. This bench of judges—two madmen and a fool—is an ironic comment on the administration of human justice. He imagines that two stools in the room are Goneril and Regan. This is the second mock trial that Lear conducts. The first is when he divides the kingdom. He is closer now to the truth about his daughters' characters. To discover this truth seems more important to him than any punishment. The warped look of the stool that is Goneril shows the material of which her heart is made. He says to Edgar that it is necessary to 'anatomise' Regan to see if there is 'any cause in nature that make these hard hearts'. Edgar and the Fool join in his fantasy in order to humour him. Edgar feels such pity for Lear that he says in an aside that his tears spoil his pretending. At Kent's suggestion, Lear decides to go to sleep. Then Gloucester hurries in. He tells Kent that there is a plot to kill the King and that Kent must drive Lear to Dover where he will find 'welcome and protection'. There is a cart ready at the door in which the King can rest. Kent must leave immediately. Any delay is dangerous. Kent, Gloucester and the Fool bear King Lear off.

Edgar remains behind. The sight of Lear's sufferings makes him feel that his own suffering is not as bad as it had seemed. He sees the similarity between Lear and himself: 'He childed as I father'd!'

NOTES AND GLOSSARY

yeoman: freeholder
bourn: brook
minikin: dainty

lym:	bloodhound
tike:	small dog
trundle-tail:	curly-tailed dog
bewray:	reveal

Act III, Scene 7

Cornwall asks Goneril to go at once to her husband, Albany, and show him the letter which Gloucester has received informing him that a French army has landed in England. He instructs his servants to find 'the traitor Gloucester'. Regan wants to 'Hang him instantly'. Goneril says 'Pluck out his eyes'. Cornwall sends Edmund to conduct Goneril home, telling him that he should not see the revenge they will take upon his father. He invests Edmund with his father's title calling him 'my Lord of Gloucester'.

Oswald enters. He informs Cornwall that Gloucester has enabled Lear to escape. Thirty-five or six of the King's knights, who had been looking for him, met him at the gate and are escorting him to Dover. Cornwall's servants bring in Gloucester. He orders them to tie Gloucester to a chair. Gloucester asks them what they mean and reminds them that they are his guests. Regan cries at him that he is a 'filthy traitor'. He answers her that he is not unmerciful as she is. Regan treats him without any respect. She pulls his beard. Gloucester rebukes her. They question him about the news he has received from France and demand to know who are his confederates and where he has sent the King. 'To Dover' is his reply. They ask why. Gloucester summons his courage and speaks to Regan: 'Because I would not see thy cruel nails / Pluck out his poor old eyes; nor see thy fierce sister' tear his sacred flesh with her 'boarish fangs'. He describes Lear's suffering in the storm and declares that he shall see vengeance overtake such children.

Cornwall declares that Gloucester will never see again. He gouges out one of his eyes. Gloucester cries out for help. Regan says that the remaining eye will mock the empty socket and encourages Cornwall to take out the other one. The horror of this is too much for one of Cornwall's servants. He tells Cornwall to stop. He says that since he was a boy he has been Cornwall's servant, and that to tell him to stop now is the best thing he has ever done for him. Cornwall draws his sword and they fight. Regan is outraged. She takes another sword and runs the man through from behind. The servant dies, but not before wounding Cornwall. Cornwall gouges out Gloucester's other eye. Gloucester moans: 'All dark and comfortless'. He calls on his son Edmund to avenge him. As the final blow, Regan tells Gloucester that Edmund hates him, and reveals to him that it is Edmund who has betrayed him. Now that he is blind, Gloucester sees the truth. He asks the Gods to forgive him. Regan tells the other servants to turn Gloucester out of the gates 'and let him smell / His way to Dover'. Then she helps Cornwall away. He is bleeding badly. The two remaining servants express their shock at the monstrous wickedness that they have witnessed. They do what they can to soothe Gloucester's wounds and decide to get the mad beggar (Edgar) to guide Gloucester.

NOTES AND GLOSSARY

festinate:	hasty
questrists:	seekers
corky:	withered
rash:	slash
stelled:	fixed
holp:	helped
dearn:	dreary

Act IV, Scene 1

Edgar, is alone, reflecting on his condition. He states that it is better to know that others condemn you than to be flattered in public and not know that you are condemned in private. The most unfortunate man lives in hope not in fear. The worst change is from the best. Any change from the worst is for the good. He welcomes the emptiness of the air. Having nothing, he owes nothing to anyone.

An old man enters leading the Duke of Gloucester. Gloucester tells the old man to leave him as he may be hurt for helping him. The old man protests that Gloucester cannot see his way. Gloucester answers that now he has no way, and that when he had eyes he could not see. If he could but touch his son Edgar whom he has wrongly treated, he would say that he could see again. The old man calls to Edgar, whom he recognises as poor Tom the mad beggar. Edgar sees what has happened to his father. He is shocked and deeply moved. He wonders how he could have thought that things were at their worst because now they are worse than ever before.

Gloucester remembers that when he met poor Tom in the hut he was reminded of his son Edgar. The Gods are like cruel boys pulling the wings off flies. They kill men for their sport. Gloucester again tells the old man to leave him. He says he will get the beggar to lead him to Dover. The old man protests that the beggar is mad. Gloucester makes this a symbol of his predicament. He replies that it is the disease of the time that madmen lead the blind. He asks Edgar if he knows the way to Dover. Edgar hesitates, wonders whether he can continue to play his part, and then decides that he must. He talks about how he has been inhabited by five fiends. Gloucester hands him a purse saying that thus his own misfortune makes Tom more fortunate. He states that the Heavens should arrange it so that the man who has more than he needs and 'that will not see / Because he does not feel', will quickly have his excess distributed to the poor so that 'each man have enough'. He asks Edgar to lead him to a cliff high above the sea at Dover where he implies that he will end his life by jumping into the sea. This is only hinted at so that the audience will understand but that the mad beggar will not. The two men go off together.

NOTES AND GLOSSARY

'parel: apparel, clothing
superfluous: having too much

Act IV, Scene 2

Goneril and Edmund have arrived at the Duke of Albany's residence. Goneril asks Oswald the whereabouts of her husband. Oswald replies that the Duke of Albany is completely changed. He smiled when he heard that the French army had landed, he said 'The worse' when told that Goneril was coming, and when informed of Gloucester's treachery and Edmund's loyalty, he stated that Oswald had things the wrong way around. On hearing this Goneril sends Edmund back to her brother-in-law, Cornwall, to urge him to hurry his preparations. Her husband is a coward. She will have to take charge of arming their men. She hints to Edmund that she will be his if he will get rid of Albany and kisses him goodbye. He leaves.

Albany enters. Goneril greets him sarcastically. Albany is not put off. He tells her that he is concerned about her character. Anyone who condemns the source of her own being as she does cannot be trusted to keep within the boundaries of right action. If she thus cuts herself off from her father she will suffer, and be murderous to others. Goneril tells him not to talk foolishness. Albany responds in even stronger terms. Wisdom and goodness seem bad only to those who are themselves bad. She and her sister have behaved like tigers, not daughters, to their father. Even a tormented bear would have been kinder than they have been. They are barbaric and degenerate. If the heavens do not intervene to stop these offences, men will become monsters.

Goneril calls him a coward. Only a fool pities a villain who is punished before he can make trouble. The French have invaded and all he does is to sit there lamenting. Albany tells her that she is a devil, and Goneril answers back that he is not a man. A messenger rushes in to tell them that the Duke of Cornwall has been killed by a servant while blinding Gloucester. This is the first that Albany has heard of the event. He is aghast. His sympathies are all with Gloucester. The messenger gives

Goneril a letter from her sister, which he says needs a speedy answer. Goneril says, speaking to herself, that in one way she is pleased by the news, imagining that with Cornwall dead she will have more power. She is unhappy, however, thinking of Regan as a widow and alone with Edmund. She goes off to answer the letter. Albany then enquires where Edmund was during all this. The messenger informs him that it was Edmund who informed against his father, and who left so that Gloucester could be punished more freely. He says that Edmund accompanied Goneril home, and that he has just passed him on his way back. Albany declares his thanks to Gloucester for what he did for the King, and states that he will try to avenge the loss of Gloucester's eyes.

NOTES AND GLOSSARY
cowish: cowardly
head-lugg'd: pulled by the head
self-covered: Goneril's monstrous behaviour has obscured her
                     human self

Act IV, Scene 3

At the French camp Kent is speaking to the gentleman that he sent as a messenger to Dover. Kent wants to know why the King of France has suddenly returned to France. The gentleman explains that there are important affairs at home with which he must deal. He tells Kent that when Cordelia read his letter about what had happened to her father tears ran down her cheeks. He describes how deeply touched she was. Kent exclaims that man must be governed by the stars, otherwise how could one father have such different daughters? He recounts to the gentleman that although King Lear is now in the French camp, he will not see Cordelia because he is so ashamed of the way that he treated her. This is a further example of how Lear allows his self-interest to override the interests of other people. Kent is still in disguise. He asks the gentleman to keep this secret.

NOTES AND GLOSSARY
one self: one and the same
make: partner

Act IV, Scene 4

Cordelia, attended by soldiers, enters with the doctor. Lear has wandered off, and they do not know where he is. Cordelia says that he has been seen only a moment before, as mad as the stormy sea, wearing a crown of weeds and singing. She orders a hundred soldiers to search the surrounding fields for him. She asks the doctor whether the King can be cured of his madness, and says that she would give everything she possesses to the man who could restore his mind. The doctor states that rest is what is needed. Cordelia urges him to find the King, because she is afraid that 'his ungovern'd rage' might cause him to take his own life. A messenger arrives with the news that the army of Goneril and Regan is marching towards them. This has been expected and Cordelia replies that they are prepared. The French are there only to aid her father, because her husband, the King of France, has taken pity on her sorrow and her tears. They are ready to fight the British army not out of any ambition, but out of love, her love for her father.

NOTES AND GLOSSARY

fumiter:	fumitory, a medicinal plant
darnel:	tares, any weed harmful to corn
century:	hundred soldiers
aidant:	helpful

Act IV, Scene 5

Oswald has brought a letter from Goneril to Edmund. Regan questions him about its contents, and about the news of her sister's camp. Oswald states that he does not know the contents of the letter. It was wrong to let Gloucester live, she says, because the sight of him sets everyone against them. Edmund has gone to put him out of his misery, and to observe the strength of the French army. Regan does not want Edmund to receive Goneril's letter. She tries to delay Oswald from going after Edmund, and when he will not, asks him to let her open the letter. He refuses. She tells him that she knows that her sister does not love her husband. The last time Goneril stayed there she gave Edmund many amorous looks. Oswald is to tell her sister that Regan's husband is dead, and that she and Edmund have come to an understanding. It is more fitting that he marry Regan than Goneril. Regan impresses upon Oswald that she wants him to make all this clear to Goneril. If he hears of 'that blind traitor' (Gloucester), anyone who kills him will be rewarded.

NOTES AND GLOSSARY

nighted:	darkened
oeilliads:	amorous looks

Act IV, Scene 6

Gloucester wants to know when they will reach the top of the high cliff overlooking the sea near Dover. Edgar pretends that they are now climbing up it. Gloucester says that the ground seems even to him. Edgar replies that it is very steep, and that the pain of his eyes must have dulled his other senses. He asks Gloucester if he hears the sea.

Gloucester says, no, but that Edgar sounds as if he is speaking in a more educated manner than before. Edgar tells him that he is deceived. Then, although they are in open country, he pretends that they are standing on the cliff. It is so high that it makes him dizzy to look down. The birds flying below them look like beetles and the fishermen walking on the beach look like mice. Gloucester insists that Edgar leads him to the very edge, then rewards him with a valuable jewel, and tells Edgar to leave him. Edgar says goodbye and walks away from him. To himself he says that he has played this game with Gloucester in the hope of curing him of his despair.

Gloucester, believing himself to be alone, prays to the Gods to allow him to rid himself of his pain, and to bless Edgar if he is alive. He throws himself forward, imagining that he is jumping off the cliff, and falls down. Edgar, assuming another voice, comes over to him and asks if he is alive or dead. 'Let me die,' says Gloucester. Edgar tells him that he has fallen from the cliff as if he was a cobweb or a feather from a height taller than the masts of ten ships. It is a miracle that he is alive. Have I really fallen? asks Gloucester. Look up, says Edgar, look up, even the noisy larks cannot be heard at such a distance. Gloucester replies that he has no eyes. He regrets that he is denied the comfort of dying, so as to put an end to his misery. Edgar describes the strange, misshapen creature he saw with Gloucester on the cliff top. He suggests that the creature was a devil, and that the Gods decided to save Gloucester's life. Edgar's cure has worked. It is almost as if Gloucester feels that he has been born again. Gloucester declares that from now on he will bear his suffering until he dies.

King Lear appears wearing his crown of weeds. To Edgar he is a heart-rending sight. Lear is talking to himself. Gloucester says, 'I know that voice'. Lear addresses him as 'Goneril, with a white beard' and continues his monologue. His daughters, he declares, flattered him 'like a dog,' but in the storm he found them out. 'Is't not the King?' says Gloucester. 'Ay, every inch a King,' replies Lear. He talks of adultery and Gloucester's bastard son as if some part of his mind knows the identity of the blind man in front of him. Should adultery be punished by death, he cries. No. Birds and insects are lustful, why should not men be so, and Gloucester's bastard son was kinder to his father than his legitimate daughters were to him. Women may pretend to be virtuous, but they have the sexual appetites of animals. Lear is still wrestling with the problem of how his daughters, his own flesh and blood, could be so cruel to him. He dwells on sexuality as if their characters were the result of something intrinsically bad in the act which brought them into being. He is trying to discover the origins of their natures.

Gloucester knows that it is King Lear and sadly recognises that he is mad. He kisses the King's hand as a sign of his obedience to the King's authority. Thus Shakespeare brings the two unfortunate fathers, both blind in different ways, face to face. Lear looks at Gloucester more carefully, and asks why he is squinting at him. 'Do thy worst, blind Cupid,' he states, 'I'll not love'. This suggests not only that part of Lear's madness is an inability to love, but that also he has wanted love from his daughters without being able to give any in return. When he asks Gloucester to read a challenge he has written, Edgar exclaims at the pathos of the situation. Gloucester answers that he has no eyes. Lear asks him if he is mad: 'A man may see how this world goes with no eyes'. If you have seen a dog chase a beggar, that is 'The great image of Authority: / A dog's obey'd in office'. This comparison has particular point since all three men after their troubles and travels look like beggars. The person who judges and punishes, Lear affirms, is as guilty as the criminal. Rich clothes hide wrongdoers and money protects sinners. If you had glass eyes, he tells Gloucester, you would be like a politician who pretends to see what he does not see.

Edgar's comment, 'O! matter and impertinency mix'd; / Reason in madness', accurately describes most of Lear's mad speeches. They combine truth, irreverence and nonsense. Shakespeare makes Lear more aware and intelligent in his madness than in his sanity.

Lear calls Gloucester by name and says he must be patient with him, but his mind wanders away to the idea of revenging himself on his sons-in-law. Some of the men sent by Cordelia to find Lear enter; they try to persuade Lear to come back with them. He runs off in the direction of the French camp, shouting for them to catch him. One of the men stays to talk with Edgar. He tells him that the battle between the armies of Goneril and Regan and the army of Cordelia is about to begin. He then leaves Gloucester and Edgar alone. Gloucester, perhaps taking note of Cordelia's loyalty to her father, and of her efforts to help him—and realising that the King is worse off than he is—asks the Gods never again to tempt him to take his own life.

Oswald comes upon them. He tells Gloucester that his eyeless head was made to raise his fortunes, and that he is going to kill him. Edgar steps between them. Oswald, thinking that he is a peasant, orders him to get out of the way. Edgar then pretends to be a peasant. He tells him in an assumed country dialect to leave them alone. Ignoring this warning, Oswald approaches with his sword ready. Edgar is armed with a staff. They fight and Oswald is mortally wounded. As he dies, he tells Edgar to deliver the letters in his purse to Edmund, Earl of Gloucester, if he wants to be rewarded. Edgar reads a letter from Goneril to Edmund, urging Edmund to kill the Duke of Albany and take his place as her husband. Edgar declares that at the right time he will show the letter to Albany. Gloucester remarks that it would be better if he himself were as mad as Lear so that he would not be conscious of his great sorrows. Edgar hears a drum. He takes Gloucester's hand and leads him towards the French camp near Dover.

NOTES AND GLOSSARY

sampire:	samphire, plant with aromatic salty leaves used in pickles
bourn:	limit
shrill-gorg'd:	shrill-voiced
whelk'd:	welked, twisted
press-money:	money paid to recruits upon enlisting
bills:	billmen, men with halberds
fitchew:	polecat
soiled:	fed with fresh-cut green fodder
handy-dandy:	take your choice (words used in a children's game)
beadle:	minor parish officer who could punish petty offenders
cozener:	cheat
zir:	sir
volk:	folk
chud:	should
che vor' ye:	I warrant you
costard:	a kind of apple, also used humorously for the head
ballow:	staff
foins:	thrusts
deathsman:	executioner
death-practis'd:	whose death is plotted

Act IV, Scene 7

Within the French camp Cordelia tells Kent that she can never thank him enough for his goodness to her father. The doctor informs Cordelia that Lear has slept long enough and that they can wake him now. The King, still asleep, is carried in and Cordelia kisses him. May her kiss, she says, repair the damage her sisters have done. Lear wakes. He tells them they should not take him out of his grave. He declares that Cordelia is a soul in paradise, while he is bound upon a wheel of fire and his tears burn like liquid lead. Lear does not know where he is. Then he kneels before Cordelia asking her not to laugh at him. His anger has disappeared. 'I am a very foolish fond old man,' he says, and he has sufficiently recovered his sanity to add: 'I fear I am not in my perfect mind'. He thinks that she is his daughter Cordelia, but he is not certain. Cordelia answers that she is, and cries. Lear says that if she has poison for him, he will drink it, because she has cause not to like him. Cordelia denies this. As Lear is confused, Cordelia and the doctor help him away. He leaves asking them to 'forget and forgive'.

NOTES AND GLOSSARY
weeds:	clothes
child-changed:	changed to a child *and* changed by his children
perdu:	soldier placed in a dangerous position

Act V, Scene 1

The battle between the British and the French is beginning. In the British camp, Edmund complains that the Duke of Albany is constantly changing his plans. Regan questions Edmund as to whether he loves Goneril. 'I never shall endure her,' she states, 'dear my Lord, / Be not familiar with her'. Goneril and Albany enter. Seeing Regan and Edmund together, Goneril immediately declares to herself that she would rather lose the battle than have Regan come between her and Edmund. Albany expresses doubts as to the justice of their cause, but they agree to forget their differences for the moment and to consult with the experienced officers about what should be done. As they leave, Edgar, still disguised, gives Albany Goneril's letter to Edmund. Read it before you fight, he directs. After the battle, if you have won, have a trumpet sounded for the man who brought it, and someone will appear to prove that what it says is true. Edmund returns with news of the enemy's strength, and sends Albany to his army.

Left by himself, Edmund reflects on what he should do. He has sworn his love to both sisters, but they are so jealous of each other that 'neither can be enjoy'd / If both remain alive.' He decides to wait until after the battle. Until then he needs the help of the Duke of Albany. If, at that point, Goneril wants Albany out of the way, she can arrange his death herself. Albany has said that he will pardon Lear and Cordelia if he captures them. Edmund is determined that they shall receive no mercy.

NOTES AND GLOSSARY
constant pleasure:	fixed decision
forfended:	forbidden
avouched:	affirmed

Act V, Scene 2

Edgar leads his father on to the stage. He tells him to wait by a tree while he goes to the battle. After a moment to indicate the passage of time, he rushes back saying that the British have lost, and that King Lear and Cordelia have been captured. Gloucester does not want to go on. Edgar reproaches him. A man must wait for death just as he waits for birth. 'Ripeness is all'. It is the readiness that matters.

Act V, Scene 3

Edmund orders his men to take King Lear and Cordelia away. Cordelia says that although they have been unlucky, she is sad only for Lear's sake. When she asks if they will see Goneril and Regan, Lear cries out 'No, no, no, no!' He tells her that in prison they will sing like birds in a cage. He imagines the happy life they will have there together. He will ask Cordelia's blessing, they will tell stories, and talk of 'the mystery of things' as if they 'were Gods' spies'.

When Lear and Cordelia have left, Edmund gives a paper on which he has written secret instructions to one of his officers. His orders must be carried out instantly, says Edmund. They are not to be questioned. Albany, Goneril and Regan enter. Albany congratulates Edmund on the victory and requests that King Lear and Cordelia be delivered to him. Edmund refuses to hand them over then and there. Albany is not pleased by this. He tells Edmund that in this war Edmund is his subordinate, not his brother or equal. Regan, who is not feeling well, quarrels with Albany on Edmund's behalf. Goneril joins in, jealous that Regan should be Edmund's defender. Regan then declares that Edmund shall be her husband. Suddenly Albany arrests Edmund and Goneril for high treason. He tells Regan that she cannot marry Edmund, because he is already promised to her sister and his wife. He does as he has been told, and orders a challenge proclaimed for anyone to come forward and prove Edmund's treason in a trial by combat. If no one comes forward, he will fight Edmund himself. He informs Edmund that he can rely only on his own valour, as all Edmund's soldiers have gone.

On the last note of the trumpet sounding the challenge, a knight appears who refuses to give his name. His face is hidden by his visor. The combat begins. Edmund falls mortally wounded. Goneril cries that this is treachery, and that Edmund was not obliged to fight an unknown opponent. Albany shows her her letter to Edmund. Goneril replies that even if she wrote it, who can judge her? The kingdom is hers; therefore, the laws belong to her. She rushes away distraught. Albany sends soldiers after her. As he is dying, Edmund confesses that he has done everything that he is charged with and more. He forgives the knight, but wants to know his identity. The knight removes his helmet and shows himself to be Edgar. Edmund says that 'The wheel has come full circle'. Edgar briefly tells the story of his disguise as a madman. He regrets that he did not tell his father who he was earlier. When he did tell him, to ask his blessing before the combat, he died. His 'flaw'd heart' broke, split between 'two extremes of passion, joy and grief'. Edgar relates that as he was crying over his father he was discovered by Kent, and that when Kent recognised who Edgar was, he told him the whole story of Lear and Gloucester and collapsed with grief.

A gentleman rushes in with a bloody knife, shouting for help. Goneril and Regan are both dead. Regan's illness was the result of having been poisoned by Goneril. Goneril, disturbed by Edmund's dying, confessed her crime and then stabbed herself. Kent enters and asks for King Lear. He has come, he says, to say good night. Albany remarks that they have forgotten about Lear. Edmund decides he wants to do 'some good'. He discloses that he has ordered the deaths of Lear and Cordelia, and urges them to hurry if they want to save them. A man runs off to countermand the order.

Lear enters carrying Cordelia in his arms. 'Howl until the sky cracks,' he cries, 'she is dead'. He places a feather on Cordelia's lips to see if she is still breathing. If she lives, he declares, that will 'redeem all sorrows'. Kent kneels to the King who pays no attention to him. Lear calls them all murderers and traitors. He might have prevented her death, but he did not, although he killed the man who was hanging her. Then Lear recognises Kent, who says that he is the same man who has been serving him under the name of Caius. Kent tells Lear that his other daughters are dead. He does not seem to understand. A messenger brings news that Edmund has died. Everyone present has been deeply affected by the succession of events. Albany announces that he will resign absolute powers to King Lear for as long as Lear lives. He will restore to Edgar and Kent their rights and add new honours. Lear interrupts, crying: 'And my poor fool is hang'd!' It is not clear whether the Fool has been hanged as well as Cordelia, or whether in his sorrow Lear is confusing the two. He asks how it is possible that dogs, horses and rats should live and not Cordelia. Then he seems to think that she is breathing again, and at that moment he dies. Let him die, says Kent, his suffering is over. It is a wonder that Lear has endured his troubles as long as he has. Albany asks Edgar and Kent to govern with him. Kent declines, saying that he must soon follow his master, Lear. Edgar states that they must all mourn and 'speak what we feel'. The young will never see so much again, 'nor live so long'. They all leave the stage.

NOTES AND GLOSSARY

fell:	skin
immediacy:	being the direct representative of someone
compeers:	equals
interlude:	play
canker-bit:	worm-eaten
maugre:	in spite of
puissant:	powerful
compliment:	ceremony
falchion:	curved sword
crosses:	troubles

Part 3

Commentary

The plot

The play lives up to its title in the First Folio; *The Tragedie of King Lear*. This is a play with one central character: King Lear.

Shakespeare tells us virtually nothing about King Lear's early life. He is interested neither in the whole of Lear's life, nor in how Lear came to be what he is when the play opens. Shakespeare focuses on a single episode at the end of Lear's life: what happens when the kingdom is divided. The King's life is summed up in the manner of his dying. He does not show us King Lear performing a variety of actions. He wants us to understand what Lear thinks and feels. Shakespeare is concerned with Lear's inner development. *The Tragedie of King Lear* is a study of mental illness. The breakup of the kingdom is followed by the breakup of Lear's mind.

Shakespeare concentrates, as he does in most of his history plays and tragedies, on one man, and that man, as is so often the case, is a king. The king is the man upon whom everything in the kingdom depends. He is especially interesting because he has the most power, the most responsibility and the most freedom. More than any other person he is able to do what he wants. He is subordinate to no one except by his own choice or failings. Shakespeare chooses the most important man in the kingdom as his major character in order to maximise the importance of the action of his play. For the same reason the tragedies usually end in death. The characters play for the highest stakes.

Shakespeare borrowed the plot of *King Lear* as he borrowed all his plots. He liked taking over someone else's story, and re-arranging and adapting it to suit his own purposes. The story of King Lear is in George Ferrers *The Mirror for Magistrates* (1574), Holinshed's *Chronicles* (1577) and Spenser's *The Faerie Queene* (1590), and there is a somewhat similar story in Sidney's *Arcadia* (1590). Shakespeare was probably familiar with all of these, but he appears to have depended most on a contemporary play, *The True Chronicle History of King Leir*, published in 1605. The author of this play is not known. There is also a record of a *kinge leare* being performed at the Rose Theatre in April 1594, but it is not certain whether this is the same play. Thus, in using the story of King Lear, Shakespeare was using a story that was known to at least some of his audience and that presents them an image of their ancient past. The play is one of three of his thirteen tragedies to be set in Britain (the others are *Macbeth* and *Cymbeline*), of which only *King Lear* and *Cymbeline* are set in England.

Like most of Shakespeare's plays, *King Lear* is divided into five acts, but the systematic division of all Shakespeare's plays into acts and scenes is the work of later editors. None of the seventeenth-century editions completely divide all the plays into acts and scenes. Some plays, like *Romeo and Juliet* and *Antony and Cleopatra*, were published without any act or scene divisions. Moreover, no edition of any of Shakespeare's plays published in his lifetime or in the seventeenth century has any stage directions as to where any scene takes place. These descriptions of place were begun by Rowe in his edition (1709) and completed by Theobald (1733) and Hanmer (1744). Occasionally in the speeches Shakespeare provides some description of where the action is taking place but his is a drama of character, not of setting.

The structure and the rhythm of the play become clearer when an outline is made of the major action of each scene (The number of lines in each act is not absolute and can vary from edition to edition.):

Act I (937 lines)
1. Lear divides his kingdom
2. Gloucester believes Edmund about Edgar
3. Goneril shows her hatred of Lear
4. Lear curses Goneril
5. Lear rejects Goneril and fears madness

Act II (634 lines)
1. Edgar flees. Gloucester's heart cracks
2. Kent abuses Oswald and is put in the stocks
3. Edgar becomes Tom
4. Regan rejects Lear. Lear goes mad

Act III (615 lines)
1. Kent looks for Lear
2. Lear wanders in the storm
3. Gloucester confides in Edmund
4. Lear confronts the disguised Edgar
5. Edmund betrays Gloucester
6. Lear tries his daughters
7. Gloucester is blinded

Act IV (686 lines)
1. Edgar encounters Gloucester
2. Albany rebukes Goneril
3. Cordelia learns of Lear's madness
4. Cordelia talks to the doctor about curing Lear
5. Regan shows her jealousy of Goneril
6. Gloucester jumps off the cliff. Lear confronts Gloucester
7. Cordelia is re-united with Lear

Act V(406 lines)   1. The battle is engaged
                                2. Edgar takes leave of Gloucester
                                3. Cordelia loses. Virtually all the major
                                    characters die

The first act in which the characters are established and the action set
in motion is the longest. The final act is the shortest. The conclusion
is decisive and comes quickly. Shakespeare's feeling for the act as a
unit of form is shown in the fact that each act comes to a climax in its
last scene. Acts I and II move more rapidly than Acts III and IV. Each
scene in the first two acts contributes a major action. The play goes
forward without any pause or interlude until Lear storms out into the
night in the last scene of the second act. After this the pace is slower
and the rhythm of the action more varied. There are no scenes in the
first two acts like that of Kent and the gentleman talking about the
King's whereabouts and the news from France (III.1) or Cordelia
talking to the doctor (IV.4). The increased number of scenes in Acts
III and IV is to take account of the increased complexity of the plot.
The characters have been scattered in small groups to a variety of
different places, and it is necessary to go from one group to another.
They are gathered together at the end as they were at the beginning.

    The tragedy is the result of the division of the kingdom. Everything
else follows from this. Shakespeare begins immediately with this decisive
event. We are plunged directly into the action. By the end of the first
scene, King Lear has divided his kingdom, he has rejected Cordelia and
Kent, Kent has suggested that he is mad, and Goneril and Regan have
agreed to co-operate. Shakespeare, however, is not very much concerned
with Lear's motives for doing this, with what has led up to this act. He
is not interested in its causes, but in its consequences.

    Shakespeare's comedies end in marriage, Shakespeare's tragedies end
in death. The final scene of *King Lear* is remarkable for the number of
deaths, most of them violent. This terrible carnage includes combat
and murder, fratricide and sororicide: Edgar kills Edmund, Gloucester
dies of a broken heart, Regan is poisoned by Goneril, Goneril kills
herself, Cordelia is murdered, the Fool is apparently hanged, and Lear
dies of a broken heart. In addition, Kent, in his last speech, speaks as
one about to die. Most revealing perhaps is that the two major protagonists, Gloucester and Lear, die of their emotions, the ultimate measure
of the intensity of their sufferings. Their feelings are literally unbearable.
Their deaths are an assertion by Shakespeare of the power of emotion.

    The violence of the final scene is not total. It is a characteristic of
Shakespeare's tragedies that there is always someone left to bury the
dead and re-establish order. Ripeness is all, but life must go on.
Shakespeare always looks to the future. Here Albany and Edgar stand

ready to pick up the pieces. Albany in his last speech orders the public mourning of the dead: 'Our present business / Is general woe,' but he is at the same time concerned with who is going to govern and how 'the gor'd state' will be sustained. Edgar, too, mourns: 'The weight of this sad time we must obey,' but he recognises that he is young, and has more to see, even if it may not equal what he has just seen.

King Lear is a play about parents and children, although there are no mothers in the play and all the children are grown up. There are, however, two fathers: Lear and Gloucester, and the plot represents the intertwining of their two stories. The outline above shows how Shakespeare alternates the story of Gloucester with that of Lear. There are not two successive scenes involving only Gloucester and his sons. More important for the structure of the play, these two stories are not separate, but complementary. When Shakespeare moves within the play from one story to another, his subject does not change. We are still seeing the difficulties of parents and children, but seeing them in relation to another set of characters. Thus, each story is a commentary on the other. The history of Gloucester is analogous to the history of Lear.

Both Lear and Gloucester are stubborn, strong-willed men who feel threatened by their children and yet who love them very much. They are both capable of deep feeling, and ill at ease with the powerful passions that they feel within themselves. They are both blind to the good and bad in their children, and both choose to trust the bad and reject the good. They both suffer because of their mistakes and are both redeemed by their suffering. The physical nature of their sufferings is a metaphor for their mental states. Lear is wise only after he becomes mad, Gloucester *sees* only after he is blind. The tragedy is that these changes come too late.

There are other correspondences in the play besides this correspondence between Lear and Gloucester. Lear has all daughters. Gloucester has all sons. Shakespeare is concerned not only with the rivalries between fathers and children, but also with the rivalries between sister and sister, and brother and brother. By making Edmund a bastard, he is able to contrast an illegitimate with a legitimate son. The king who is foolish is confronted again and again with the fool who is wise. There is a father who goes mad and a son who only pretends to go mad. They, too, are brought face to face. At times they vaguely resemble each other: Lear bedraggled by the storm or bedecked with weeds suggests Edgar disguised as Tom. Moreover, there are two men in disguise: Kent and Edgar. The hypocrites in the play, Goneril, Regan and Edmund, disguise their loyalties, but Kent and Edgar disguise themselves in order to remain loyal.

Correspondences like this are a characteristic of all Shakespeare's plots and derive from his desire to look at everything from as many points of view as possible. He repeats situations and relationships in the same way that he repeats metaphors. The structures of Shakespeare's plots show the same habits of mind as his metaphor-making.

These correspondences are, of course, only *partial* symmetries: Lear has three children, Gloucester has two; Gloucester has an illegitimate child, Lear does not. Shakespeare does not want everything completely balanced or regular. He wants only enough to knit the plot together and to explore fully the subject that he is considering.

The characters

Shakespeare's characters reveal themselves by what they say and do on the stage. They tell us more by their speeches than by their actions, but Kent's readiness for action is shown more by his tripping Oswald than by his previous words to Lear (I.4) and no words could show us Cornwall's spiteful rage and amoral ruthlessness like his determination to put out both Gloucester's eyes (III.7). That he does this himself and does not merely threaten to do it or order someone else to do it, is what reveals his character to us. We also learn about individual characters from how the other characters behave to them and from what they say about them. Weighing what one character says about another demands great care, because any such speech reflects both upon the character described and upon the speaker. When Regan says that Lear 'hath ever but slenderly known himself' (I.1.293–4), we cannot be certain that she is not speaking primarily out of jealousy and anger. It is only towards the end of the play that we can see the truth and significance of this statement.

The most significant events in Shakespeare's tragedies are the changes that take place in the major characters. His protagonists strive for contact with reality. They struggle to know themselves and the world. The tragedies show them at a crisis in the process of changing, facing a turning-point in themselves. Their struggle for self-knowledge is usually a struggle between their old self and the new.

The interaction of characters is an agent of change. Shakespeare excels at bringing his major characters together at decisive moments. Each tragedy is a series of confrontations. The action of *King Lear* begins with Lear confronting all three of his daughters and rejecting Cordelia before the assembled court. Next Goneril rejects Lear and then Regan rejects him. The two mad men (Lear and Edgar) and the two blind men (Lear and Gloucester) are brought face to face. The others act as mirrors in which Lear can see himself. At the end Lear's meetings with Cordelia complete the change in his character.

What the characters say to each other enables us to know or guess what they are feeling, but Shakespeare is not satisfied with only showing the outside. His concern with inner states is shown by his use of the aside and the soliloquy. Through these two techniques the audience is directly informed of exactly what the characters are thinking.

King Lear

The character of King Lear is complex. He is not a character with a single tragic flaw. During the play King Lear changes in a deep and radical way. Through great torment and the endless jar of right and wrong, he comes to a better knowledge of himself and the world. He starts as a man who throughout a long life 'hath ever but slenderly known himself' (I.1.293–4). At the end he is able to accept what he is and to admit his weaknesses:

> I am a very foolish fond old man,
> Fourscore and upward, not an hour more nor less;
> And, to deal plainly,
> I fear I am not in my perfect mind.
> (IV.7.60–3)

This self-knowledge is a sign that he is recovering his sanity. His most complete moment of happiness occurs when he is reconciled with Cordelia and looking forward to being with her (V.3.8–19; 20–6). It is followed almost immediately by his most profound moment of sorrow, when his new understanding with Cordelia comes to an abrupt end with her murder (V.3.257–311). He dies of a broken heart.

The energy of his speeches makes it possible to forget that King Lear is a very old man, especially for Shakespeare's time. He is over eighty, and it is under the pressure of growing old that he decides to divide his kingdom. He wants to unburden himself of the 'cares and business' (I.1.39) of government and keep only 'the name and all th' addition' (I.1.136), the prestige, honours, titles and ceremonies. This is a tragic mistake, even apart from the rejection of Cordelia, and Shakespeare appropriately has King Lear refer to it as his 'darker purpose' (I.1.36). This fatal decision is very much Lear's free choice, determined not by any outside force, but by his character. Shakespeare emphasises this by having Kent and the Fool tell the King over and over in the first two acts that he has done the wrong thing. Not only does Lear not see for himself, he ignores all the warnings of others. This is not simple stubbornness, but a denial of reality that is the beginning of his madness.

For Shakespeare, the division of a kingdom means civil war and is an image of chaos. Power cannot be separated from responsibility. That Lear believes this is possible is one of the many ways in which he is out of touch with reality. That he seeks to enjoy the pleasures of power without accepting its pains is an indication of his selfishness.

King Lear is self-centred, pre-occupied throughout the play with his own predicament and his own feelings. He is child-like in his manner of wanting his own way and in wanting to destroy the world when it does not conform to his wishes (see III.1.1–9). Only after his madness, when he has taken leave of his former self, does he begin to show concern for other people, as when he is concerned that the Fool is cold (III.2.68) and when he thinks of all the 'poor naked wretches' who are suffering in the storm (III.4.23–36). Here his concern for others is marked by his urging Kent and the Fool to go into the hovel before him, behaviour rare in a king. Nevertheless, even when he is at last reconciled with Cordelia, he has difficulty in saying that he is sorry, although he does admit he has done her wrong in a roundabout way (IV.7.72–5). He asks Cordelia not to mock him or laugh at him or abuse him, but it is not until later that he asks outright for forgiveness (IV.7.84–85). When he speaks to Cordelia about it again he presents it as happening in the future (V.3.10–11).

Lear has a desperate need to be loved. It is his daughters' ingratitude that he finds most bitter. To Goneril he says: 'How sharper than a serpent's tooth it is / To have a thankless child!' (I.1.297–8) and he speaks of 'Monster Ingratitude!' (I.5.40). The private fact of love is not enough for him; he demands a public statement of his daughters' affections and even wants them to compete with each other in their declarations. He does not offer affection to them, only the command: love me. As it is in the nature of love that it can only be freely given, it is not surprising that all three daughters, in their different ways, evade his command.

Lear's need to be loved is so great that he not only threatens, cajoles and pleads with his daughters to care for him, but also studiously ignores the true nature of their behaviour. He pretends that the world is other than it is. Perhaps the clearest example of Lear's denial of reality is when he says no again and again to Kent, refusing to believe that Cornwall and Regan had him put in the stocks (II.4.12–27).

The desire for love and this denial of reality are related in Lear to his inability to feel and to his resistance to sorrow. His misjudgments of others seem to come about because he cannot enter into their feelings. His will is at war with his deepest feelings. He fights in the first two acts any show of emotion except anger. When Goneril wants to reduce his train he affirms:

> *I am asham'd*
> *That thou hast power to shake my manhood thus,*
> *That these hot tears, which break from me perforce,*
> *Should make thee worth them.*
>
> (I.4.305–8)

He resists weeping in the most savage terms:

> *Old fond eyes,*
> *Beweep this cause again, I'll pluck ye out,*
> *And cast you, with the waters that you loose,*
> *To temper clay.*
>
> (I.4.310–13)

When he finally accepts that Cornwall and Regan have imprisoned Kent in the stocks, he feels overcome by sadness and he cries out:

> *O! how this mother swells up toward my heart;*
> *Hysterica passio! down, thou climbing sorrow!*
> *Thy element's below.*
>
> (II.4.56–8)

Finding that Goneril and Regan are united against him, he describes himself as 'a poor old man / As full of grief as age,' but he will not cry the tears that he feels:

> *. . . fool me not so much*
> *To bear it tamely; touch me with noble anger,*
> *And let not women's weapons, water-drops,*
> *Stain my man's cheeks! . . .*
> *. . . You think I'll weep;*
> *No, I'll not weep:*
> *I have full cause of weeping, but this heart*
> *Shall break into a hundred thousand flaws*
> *Or ere I'll weep. O Fool! I shall go mad.*
>
> (II.4.274–88)

The choice is made explicit in this speech: either to weep or to go mad. King Lear chooses madness.

Throughout the first half of the play, Lear is possessed by a 'great rage'. It is only when this is past that the Doctor sees a chance of his recovery (IV.7.78–9). Before this Lear literally keeps losing his temper, that is, he loses all his moderation. Shakespeare shows us in *King Lear* the full sense of the word *madness*, which means both anger and insanity. Lear's anger develops into insanity. After going mad, Lear gradually begins to re-absorb the world. He starts to see his daughters as they are. He accepts the help of Kent. He is more considerate of the Fool and treats poor Tom O'Bedlam with the greatest seriousness. The mock trial of Goneril and Regan (III.4) represents a mitigation of Lear's fury, as it shows him at least attempting to forsake his savage desire for private revenge, and to re-impose in his life the processes of order and law. His murderous desires continue to break out (see IV.6.185–9) until after his reconciliation with Cordelia.

Despite all of his weaknesses, King Lear inspires great loyalty, not only in Cordelia, but in the Fool, Kent and Gloucester. All risk their lives to aid Lear; they stand by him even when he rejects them. They recognise the good in him and serve to remind us of it. That Lear is not betrayed by his friends, that throughout the play he is surrounded by people ready to help him, shows us that his struggle is primarily with himself. He is responsible for his fate.

His madness causes Lear to question his own nature and that of the world. When in the first scene of the play Cordelia refuses to say anything, Lear does not inquire into her motives, but only asks if she means it and then, when she says she does, denounces her. Later, as he feels what it is to be without power, he changes. Defending the number of his train, he states that a man's true needs are other than what he needs merely to survive (II.4.266–72), and in the storm he wonders who preserves 'Poor naked wretches' against the elements (III.4.28–36). He confesses: 'O I have ta'en / Too little care of this'. These thoughts are developed further as a result of his encounter with the disguised Edgar. He sees the miserable Tom O'Bedlam as representing the true nature of man: 'thou art the thing itself; unaccommodated man is no more but such a poor, bare, forked animal as thou art' (III.4.109–10).

Lear asks Edgar: 'What is the cause of thunder?' (III.4.159). This is not only a question about the nature of the world, but also an indirect request for knowledge of the storm within himself. He calls Edgar 'my philosopher' and wants to continue his conversation with him, as if thereby he could get to the bottom of everything. It is to Edgar that he subsequently addresses the question that troubles him so deeply, why his daughters have been so unloving to him: 'Is there any cause in nature that makes these hard hearts?' (III.6.78–9). It is their ingratitude that provokes his bitter reflections on the nature of justice (IV.6.151–75). As part of his search for self-knowledge, Lear re-examines the society in which he lives.

Goneril and Regan

Shakespeare does not distinguish much between the characters of Goneril and Regan. They are very alike. Regan defines herself in terms of Goneril: 'I am made of that self metal as my sister, / And prize me at her worth.' (I.1.69–70) and her behaviour often copies Goneril's.

Goneril, King Lear's eldest daughter, appears stronger than Regan. It is she who at the end of Scene 1 approaches Regan and suggests that they work together against Lear. The difference between their characters can be observed in the last lines of this scene. Regan agrees with Goneril, saying: 'We shall further think of it'. Goneril wants immediate action: 'We must do something, and i' th' heat'.

Goneril is the leader of those allied against Lear, at least until Edmund takes command. She opposes Lear before Regan although Cordelia resists him before either of them. She orders Oswald to provoke Lear (I.3). She meets her father squarely without hesitation, and bears the brunt of his anger and his terrible curse without flinching (I.4). When Lear leaves her, she writes at once to Regan telling her what to do and Regan follows her directions (I.4.341–50). Goneril appears all the stronger because of the way in which she dominates her husband in the first three acts of the play and when Albany rejects her she seems all the more vicious because of his change of heart. Regan is not as strong as her husband. She follows him as she follows Goneril. Gloucester refers to the stubbornness and 'fiery quality' of the Duke of Cornwall (II.4.92–4).

At the beginning of King Lear's visit (II.4) Regan is milder with her father than Goneril has been. She becomes direct and ruthless only after Goneril arrives (II.4.203–8), as if taking courage from her sister's presence, and it is she who orders that the gates of Gloucester's house be closed, shutting Lear out in the storm (II.4.306). After this, the pace at which the two sisters become more and more savage seems to quicken. Goneril remains the more ferocious. When Gloucester's treason is discovered, Regan cries: 'Hang him instantly'. It is Goneril who says: 'Pluck out his eyes' (III.7.4–5). Regan, however, pulls Gloucester's beard when his arms are tied (III.7.35–6), and encourages Cornwall and taunts Gloucester while Cornwall blinds him. She is not only completely unmoved by this, but she still feels vindictive. She orders the servants: 'Go thrust him out at gates, and let him smell / His way to Dover' (III.7.92–3).

Goneril and Regan are jealous and greedy. As they are jealous of Cordelia because she had most of their father's love (I.1.290), because of Edmund they become jealous of each other. Each seeks to prevent the other from enjoying Edmund's love, not so much for Edmund's sake as for spite. Goneril declares: 'I had rather lose the battle than that sister / Should loosen him and me' (V.1.18–19). Regan, in this same scene, cannot bear that Goneril and Edmund should be alone together for a moment. For Goneril and Regan love is a matter of intrigue and falsity. They pretend to love their father in order to gain control of the kingdom. They pretend to love each other in order to obtain Edmund's love. The unnatural daughters are attracted to the unnatural son.

They are greedy in that they want everything now. Despite King Lear's age, they cannot wait to enjoy his power. Similarly, neither sister can wait to become Edmund's wife. They each make advances to him. Their desire is a greedy lust. Throughout the play the two sisters are frequently described in terms of animal metaphors, and usually the animals are carnivorous with sharp claws or teeth. Lear addresses

Goneril as 'detested kite' (I.4.271) and refers to her 'wolvish visage' (I.4.317). Albany says that they are 'Tigers, not daughters' (IV.2.40). These are images of greed. Shakespeare sees Goneril and Regan turning upon their father in a savage and cannibalistic rage.

Goneril's behaviour is more extreme than Regan's. Regan's interest in Edmund may be unseemly so soon after her husband's death, but Goneril's passion for him is adulterous and she goes even further in urging Edmund to kill her husband (IV.2.19–21; IV.6.264–72). She poisons her sister (V.3.96–7; V.3.226–7) and kills herself. Thus Goneril violates most of the closest human relationships (those of daughter, sister and wife) and she is unable to respect even her own self.

Cordelia

Cordelia is King Lear's favourite daughter. As he rejects her, Lear speaks of his dream of spending his old age with Cordelia and her children: 'I lov'd her most, and thought to set my rest / On her kind nursery' (I.1.122–3). Goneril states that 'he always lov'd our sister most' (I.1.290) and both she and Regan interpret Lear's rejection of Cordelia as proof that his judgment is gone. This is also Kent's opinion (I.1.144–54) and even the King of France, a visitor to the court, knows that Cordelia:

> even but now was your best object,
> The argument of your praise, balm of your age,
> The best, the dearest . . .'

> (I.1.214–16)

If Goneril and Regan embody their father's selfishness, Cordelia has his wilfulness. In her stubborn refusal to speak of her love, she is very much her father's daughter. The scrupulousness involved in this refusal suggests her youth and inexperience, but she is unable to bear her sisters' falseness and is concerned to differentiate herself from them. On the eve of her marriage she is conscious of the tug between her feelings for her father and for her husband (I.1.99–104). Perhaps it is because he is dimly aware of this that Lear insists so vigorously that she pledge her allegiance to him. He dotes on her to such an extent, and in such a way, that the smallest departure from his wishes seems an ugly and serious fault (compare I.4.275–81). It is as if Cordelia must conform to his fantasy of what his daughter ought to be. This amounts to a denial of her chance to be herself.

Cordelia's love for her father is unchanged by the break. She does not answer anger with anger. Her desire to aid her father causes her to engage a French army in England (see III.1.17–49, III.4.10–15 and IV.5.23–9). She cries when she hears the news of him in France

(IV.5.25–6) and she cries when she reads Kent's letter (IV.3.10–33). Her ready tears can be contrasted with Lear's struggle against his sorrow. All Cordelia's energies are devoted to the restoration of Lear. To this end she is prepared to give all that she possesses. She tells the doctor that: 'He that helps him take all my outward worth' (IV.4.10). She puts the highest value on loyalty. She tells Kent:

> O thou good Kent! how shall I live and work
> To match thy goodness? My life will be too short,
> And every measure fail me.
>
> (IV.7.1–3)

Her last speech expresses this same selflessness (V.3.3–7). She is indifferent to her defeat except as it may affect Lear.

The Fool

For all their individuality and the vividness of their characters, there is a sense in which Goneril, Regan, Cordelia, the Fool and Kent can be considered as adjuncts to the character of Lear. This is especially true of the Fool. The first we hear of him, Lear has struck one of Goneril's gentlemen (not a servant!) for scolding his Fool (I.3.1–2). The Fool's closeness to Lear is emphasised by the fact that he, too, is particularly fond of Cordelia. One of the knights remarks that 'Since my young Lady's going into France, Sir, the Fool hath much pined away' (I.4.77–8).

The Fool enters in Act I, Scene 4, only after the division of the kingdom and after Lear has become aware that he is being badly treated by Goneril. He exits in Act III, Scene 6, when he helps Kent and Gloucester put Lear in the litter that is to take him to Dover. At this point the Fool is no longer necessary. The first rage of Lear's madness has passed and he is beginning to be more or less in touch with reality. As Lear decides to go in out of the storm, he acquires a new dignity. The mock trial represents an effort to re-establish order in the kingdom of his mind. Up to this point the Fool has constantly tried to make Lear understand what he has done. His language, a combination of rhymes and songs, paradoxes and puns, is unlike that of any other character. His purpose is to make the King see the world as it is and to help him to laugh at his terrors. When Kent asks who is with Lear in the storm, the gentleman replies: 'None but the Fool, who labours to out-jest / His heart-strook injuries' (III.1.16–17).

The Fool is the companion of Lear's madness and like the son he never had. He is Lear's *alter ego* and speaks to him with the voice of conscience. When King Lear is foolish, the Fool is wise, but, as the sorrow deepens, the Fool is out of place. There is no laughter in the final acts of *King Lear* and the obvious absence of the Fool makes the tragedy all the darker.

The Earl of Kent

Kent is a study in loyalty and anger. He is the only character in the play who stands by Lear from the beginning of the King's troubles until his death. (The Fool is equally loyal, but he is present neither at the first scene nor at the conclusion.) Kent's profession of loyalty is complete:

> Royal Lear,
> Whom I have ever honour'd as my King,
> Lov'd as my father, as my master follow'd,
> As my great patron thought on in my prayers,
>
> (I.1.139–42)

Nothing could be simpler than his exchange with Lear when he seeks employment as a servant:

LEAR: *What wouldst thou?*
KENT: *Service.*
LEAR: *Who wouldst thou serve?*
KENT: *You*   (I.4.24–7)

He is determined to serve Lear despite the order for his banishment with its threat of death if he is found out. His comment after Lear's death reveals the depth of his loyalty and his capacity for feeling: 'I have a journey, sir, shortly to go; / My master calls me, I must not say no' (V.3.321–2). His loyalty is a yardstick by which all the other characters are measured. Gloucester appears a politician next to Kent. Albany's vacillation is especially marked. Cordelia feels that she has been disloyal when she meets Kent at Dover (see IV.7.1–3).

Kent is a man of action. He intervenes without any hesitation in the division of the kingdom. He is prepared to perform all the tasks necessary to be Lear's servant. He trips Oswald when Oswald is rude to Lear and fights with him the next time that he sees him. He has the strength to confront Lear at the height of Lear's anger against Cordelia. He calls Lear 'old man,' tells him that he is mad and that his conduct is 'folly'. He implores Lear to check his 'hideous rashness' (I.1.146–54). He is vehement, blunt and direct, courageous and passionate. He lives up to his description of himself to Cornwall: 'tis my occupation to be plain' (II.2.93; compare I.4.35–6). Kent resembles Cordelia in that he finds 'the glib and oily art' of hypocrites unbearable (compare I.1.223–33 and II.2.73–81).

Kent finds it difficult to check his own temper. He does not appear to restrain himself when defending Cordelia in the opening scene. There is nothing in the play to compare to his invective against Oswald (II.2.1–96), and even a less bad-tempered man than the Duke of Cornwall would have taken offence at Kent's statement:

> I have seen better faces in my time
> Than stands on any shoulder that I see
> Before me at this instant.

(II.2.94–6)

(especially as Regan, Cornwall's wife, was present). Certainly Kent's behaviour in this scene does not do his master, Lear, any good. His anger, however, is soon over. He faces a night in the stocks with unruffled equanimity and without bitterness. The humour of his abuse of Oswald also shows his good nature. This element in his anger distinguishes him from the other angry men in the play, Lear and Cornwall. Perhaps this is why, unlike them, Kent goes neither mad nor wrong.

The Earl of Gloucester

Gloucester seems a man overwhelmed by events. He watches his ordered world go to pieces without understanding why (I.2.23–6 and I.2.107–23). Consequently he is swept along by these 'ruinous disorders' and led by others until it is too late. He is utterly dismayed by what Edmund tells him about Edgar, but forms no plan of his own. He follows Edmund's directions. Similarly, he accepts Cornwall as: 'The noble Duke, my master, / My worthy arch and patron' (II.1.58–9) and confides his sorrow to Regan (II.1.90), although he does what he can to prevent Kent being put in the stocks (II.2.140–7). He apologises to Kent (II.2.152–4), temporises with Lear (II.4.91–120), and only hints that Lear should not be shut out in the storm (II.4.302–4). He tries vainly to heal the divisions in the kingdom and to have things both ways. He tells Lear: 'I would have all well betwixt you' (III.4.120), but he appears set to obey Cornwall until he learns that the French army has invaded (III.4).

Gloucester sees the impending chaos, but he is blind to the characters of his two sons. Whether or not Edmund can hear his father's remarks in the opening scene of the play, Gloucester speaks of him in a very impersonal and casual way. The first scene almost makes it appear as if Gloucester's blindness is punishment for his lust, but it is more accurate to say that his punishment is the result of his blindness. He says: 'I have so often blush'd to acknowledge him, that now I am braz'd to't' (I.1.9–11). He is ashamed of Edmund and has hardened himself so as not to feel his shame. Like Lear he resists his feelings, and like Lear he dies of a broken heart. When they find out what they have done, Lear goes mad, Gloucester tries to kill himself. Gloucester, however, does find his courage when he is questioned by Cornwall and Regan (II.7). Although he is completely in their power, he behaves with dignity and testifies to his loyalty to Lear. He also finds the courage with Edgar's help to go on living despite his wretchedness. He is a wiser man after his blindness, but his wisdom is the wisdom of sorrow. He changes during the play, but not enough to survive the shock of discovering that Edgar has been his companion. He dies, as Edgar says, 'twixt two extremes of passion', his joy at being reunited with his loyal son, and his grief for the wrong he has done him (V.3.196–9).

Edgar

Edgar is the Earl of Gloucester's legitimate son, older than Edmund, the heir to his title and property and the recipient, except for a brief period, of all his father's love. He does not resemble his father in any particular way. He does not know his illegitimate brother very well, although he seems to treat him in an ordinary, friendly and open way (I.2.145–91). Edmund has been away for the nine years before the opening scene, and is, until the kingdom is divided, about to go away again (I.1.32–3). Instead it is Edgar who is forced to hide. Kent is banished and Edgar is proclaimed (II.3.1–21). As a result of King Lear's abdication of responsibility, both loyal and honest men must disguise themselves in order to survive.

Edgar becomes Tom O'Bedlam. As the King is reduced to wandering the countryside in a storm, this nobleman's son, the heir to an earldom, is reduced to smearing himself with dirt, discarding all his clothes except a blanket and pretending to be mad. The Fool says to Lear: 'I am a Fool, thou art nothing' (I.4.202). Edgar declares: 'Edgar I nothing am' (II.4.21). They, like Kent in the stocks (II.3.173), exemplify the turning of Fortune's wheel, the vicissitudes of life.

If Goneril represents the barbarism of civilisation, Edgar, disguised as a mad beggar, represents 'unaccommodated man,' man stripped of virtually every vestige of civilisation. His madness makes him seem scarcely human, and in his nakedness and poverty he lives virtually like an animal. He says that he 'eats the swimming frog, the toad, the tadpole, the wall-newt' and 'drinks the green mantle of the standing pond' (III.4.132–7). Lear recognises this when he calls him 'a poor, bare, forked animal' (III.4.110). Goneril shows us the moral abyss, Edgar the abyss of physical suffering. No one in the play sinks any lower physically than Edgar. His madness is feigned, but the hardships of his outlawed life are real.

Edgar takes courage from feeling that nothing worse can happen to him, until he meets his father with his eyes gone and the empty sockets bleeding (IV.1.1–9; 24–8) and witnesses mad Lear's conversation with blind Gloucester (IV.6.142–3).

Like the Fool, Edgar as poor Tom speaks a special language, more extreme and fantastical than that of the Fool, even crazier than Lear. Edgar, in fact, makes Lear seem saner. As a result, Edgar and the Fool are the two characters who seem best able to communicate with King Lear at the height of his madness.

When the disguise of mad Tom has served its purpose, Edgar abandons it (IV.6.66–74), and pretends to be a peasant. At the end of the play he ceases to be his father's escort, and becomes his avenger. He kills Edmund, his father's betrayer and the leader of the armies against Lear. He also kills Oswald and gives Albany the letter that proves Goneril's treachery. He becomes the agent of justice and order.

Edmund

Edmund is the younger and natural or illegitimate son of the Earl of Gloucester. His father is ashamed of his existence (I.1.9–11) and apparently has kept him abroad for the past nine years (I.1.32). Energetic and ambitious, he feels that he has been denied the advantages to which his appearance and abilities ought to entitle him. He declares: 'Thou, Nature, art my goddess' and rejects the customs of the society that has rejected him (I.2.1–22). Thus, he sees himself as virtually an outlaw, and sets himself in opposition to legitimacy and to the established order. He proceeds with vigour, speed and total ruthlessness to drive his brother Edgar from his father's house, and then to convict his father of treason so as to receive his title and lands. He is indifferent to the fact that this leads to the blinding of his father, and when he learns that the appearance of Gloucester turns people against him, he rides out to kill him if he can (IV.5.8–14).

Like Goneril and Regan, Edmund is completely selfish, while pretending to loyalties that he does not feel. His behaviour contrasts with that of Goneril and Regan in that his is the amorality of nature, while theirs is the amorality of culture, of legitimate daughters living within the family and the law. They are, however, alike in their evilness. Lear calls Goneril 'Degenerate bastard' (I.4.262), and says to Regan that he would think that she is illegitimate if she were not glad to see him (II.4.130–3). He calls them 'unnatural hags' (II.4.280) when they have both rejected him. The similar nature of Goneril, Regan and Edmund is confirmed when they become allies and by the way in which the two sisters are attracted to Edmund. Edmund, however, has no feelings for them and merely uses them as he does everyone else (V.2.55–65).

Edmund has the courage of his amorality. He mocks the idea that the stars are in any way responsible for his character (I.2.124–40). At the end, he accepts without hesitation responsibility for all his evil actions (V.3.161–4). Edmund is, moreover, not absolutely evil. He forgives Edgar for killing him even before he knows who he is and admits that he is moved by Edgar's account of their father's death (V.3.181–200). Finally, he decides to do 'some good' despite his nature. He tells Albany and Edgar of the danger to Lear and Cordelia, and urges them three times to send quickly to save their lives (V.3.243–6). Like so much in *King Lear*, this change of heart comes too late.

Metaphors and images

Aristotle* states in the *Poetics* (1459a) that the greatest thing is to be a master of metaphor. All art is metaphor: the expression of one thing in terms of another. Shakespeare's plays cannot be defined by a summary of the action. He borrowed all his plots. His contribution is the language, the interpretation. Shakespeare's greatness resides in the exact way in which he says things.

Each play of Shakespeare is the development of a metaphor or group of metaphors. There is a matrix out of which feeling finds words, emotions take shape and voices become characters. That which is referred to most often—in metaphors, images, allusions and statements—is usually for Shakespeare what is most significant. We have not understood a play unless we have understood all its repeated metaphors and the connections between them. Shakespeare's plays are unified through their metaphors. He explores an idea by transforming it many times.

King Lear opens with the division of a kingdom. This is enacted in the first scene, and in the second scene Gloucester makes it into a metaphor that comprehends most of the action of the play:

> These late eclipses in the sun and moon portend no good to us:
> though the wisdom of Nature can reason it thus and thus, yet Nature
> finds itself scourg'd by the sequent effects. Love cools, friendship
> falls off, brothers divide: in cities, mutinies; in countries, discord; in
> palaces, treason; and the bond crack'd 'twixt son and father. This
> villain of mine comes under the prediction; there's son against father:
> the King falls from bias of nature; there's father against child. We
> have seen the best of our time: machinations, hollowness, treachery,
> and all ruinous disorders follow us disquietly to our graves.
>
> (I.2.107–20)

* Aristotle (384-322 BC), Greek philosopher.

This speech generalises the significance of what has just happened and foreshadows what is to come. The actions of Lear and Edgar are seen as involving the whole universe: cities, countries, the sun and the moon. The family is an image of the kingdom and the kingdom is an image of the world and all human life. This speech is Shakespeare's way of making explicit to the audience that the action of his play is symbolic. More specifically, it states that the story of Edmund and Edgar ('brothers divided') and that of Gloucester and his son ('there's son against father') are analogous to the story of Lear and Cordelia ('there's father against child'), that they are all ways of looking at the same subject: the relations between members of the same family.

The idea of things cracking, splitting and breaking can be followed throughout the play—and in some of the most important speeches. After Gloucester is convinced of Edgar's treachery, he cries to Regan: 'O! Madam, my old heart is crack'd, its crack'd' (II.1.90) and Lear, when he is at last persuaded that both his daughters have forsaken him, declares:

> *I have full cause of weeping, but this heart*
> *Shall break into a hundred thousand flaws*
> *Or ere I'll weep. O Fool! I shall go mad.*
> (II.4.286–8)

Flaw here is a fragment, but it also means *crack* and *defect*. Shakespeare brings all three senses to bear in this context. This is a good example of how rich his words are with meaning and of the power and exactness with which he uses them. He employs the same word again in Edgar's description of Gloucester's death:

> *his flaw'd heart,*
> *Alack, too weak the conflict to support!*
> *'Twixt two extremes of passion, joy and grief,*
> *Burst smilingly.*
> (V.3.196–9)

In the storm Lear shouts: 'Blow, winds, and crack your cheeks! rage! blow!' (III.2.1) and 'close pent-up guilts, rive your concealing continents' (III.2.57–8). He imagines all nature splitting like his own mind. He is unable either to feel or to contain his emotions and goes mad. Like Gloucester, Lear is caught in the conflict between two extremes of passion, in his case: anger and grief. The storm outside is equal to the storm inside.

Most of our words for madness have to do with splitting or loss of shape or form. We say that a mad person is *cracked*. *Crazy* means full of cracks. We also say that a person has a *breakdown* or that he is *all broken up* as the result of feeling some powerful emotion. *Heartbreak* is another word for sorrow. Edgar says, as he watches mad Lear and blind Gloucester: 'it is and my heart breaks at it' (IV.6.142–3). Albany says to Edmund: 'Let sorrow split my heart, if ever I / Did hate thee or thy father' (V.3.176–7). Edgar describes Kent when he told him of what had happened to Lear: 'in recounting / His grief grew puissant, and the strings of life / Began to crack' (V.3.215–17).

The splitting of the kingdom involves the drawing of boundaries. Shakespeare in *King Lear* is concerned with the boundary between the natural and the unnatural, between justice and injustice.

The division of the kingdom provides us with an image of justice gone wrong. The King makes a trial of his three daughters, he conducts a second trial during the storm in Act III, Scene 6, and we see justice done at the end of the play, including a trial by combat between Edgar and Edmund. There are, moreover, a number of speeches about justice in the play. The wretch who has within himself 'undivulged crimes / Unwhipp'd of Justice' (III.2.51–3) should tremble, says Lear in the storm and in the same speech he uses the legal term 'perjur'd'. Cornwall when he orders Gloucester brought before him thinks that he ought not to punish him without a trial: 'Though well we may not pass upon his life / Without the form of justice' (III.7.24–5). Lear's conversation with Gloucester when they meet on the road to Dover is mostly about justice. He emphasises how difficult it is to tell 'which is the justice and which is the thief' (IV.6.152–6). *King Lear* is about justice in that the characters both discuss justice and enact it. We see metaphors as well as hear them.

Both Lear and Gloucester change the division of their land among their children. They draw new boundaries, and Cordelia and Edgar are left for a time with nothing. *Nothing* is a word used over and over in different contexts throughout the play. Shakespeare employs it to help describe what we call identity, as when the Fool says to Lear: 'now thou art an O without a figure. I am better than thou art now; I am a Fool, thou art nothing' (I.4.200–2) or Edgar when he becomes Tom: 'Edgar I nothing am' (II.3.21).

Lear when he rejects Cordelia declares:

> Here I disclaim all my paternal care,
> Propinquity and property of blood,
> And as a stranger to my heart and me
> Hold thee from this for ever. The barbarous Scythian,
> Or he that makes his generation messes
> To gorge his appetite, shall to my bosom
> Be as well neighbour'd, pitied, and reliev'd,
> As thou my sometime daughter.
>
> (I.1.113–20)

The phrase 'property of blood' makes us aware of the division of land. The forces that bring about Lear's madness are at work here. Lear splits himself from his heart or feelings when he refers to: 'my heart and me'. With the Scythian and 'he that makes his generation messes' (*messes*: portions of food), Lear introduces the notion of cannibalism twice—in the future, a cannibal, he says, will be as close to me as you.

Cannibalism is the most primitive form of aggression. It is common in children's stories; the giant is always saying to the hero: 'I am going to eat you up.' Cannibalism is one of the ordinary feelings of the baby at the mother's breast (note that Lear says 'to my bosom / Be'). Shakespeare keeps recurring to the idea. When Lear explains why he does not mind the storm, he says:

> But where the greater malady is fix'd,
> The lesser is scarce felt. Thou'ldst shun a bear;
> But if thy flight lay toward the roaring sea,
> Thou'ldst meet the bear i' th' mouth.
>
> (III.4.8–11)

And a moment later, he exclaims:

> filial ingratitude!
> Is it not as this mouth should tear this hand
> For lifting food to 't
>
> (III.4.14–16)

The image of his children biting the hand that fed them has already begun to take shape in his thoughts of meeting 'the bear i' th' mouth.' The same idea is repeated in the epithet: 'Those pelican daughters' (III.4.75) because the mother pelican, according to many old books, by piercing her breast with her bill fed her young with her own blood.

The ingratitude of children in *King Lear* is conceived as cannibalistic. This is one reason why there are so many references to monsters (including dragons) which are fantastic, barbarous, unnatural creatures and why Lear speaks of 'Monster ingratitude' (I.5.40)—why 'How sharper than a serpent's tooth it is to have a thankless child!' (I.4.297–8), and why Regan and Goneril are again and again compared to animals with sharp teeth, especially carnivorous predators: foxes, wolves, dogs, tigers and 'the sharp tooth'd ... vulture' (II.4.136)—and how they fit neatly together with 'treason's tooth' (V.3.122) and that curious expression 'Lipsbury pinfold' (II.2.9) which suggests a paper of pins and a mouth full of teeth. (A pinfold is a place or pen where stray cattle or sheep are confined.)

It is a characteristic of Shakespeare that during the course of a play he turns the same set of metaphors and images over and over in his mind, considering them from different points of view, combining and recombining them. The ideas of the division of the kingdom and the cracking of the King's mind, nothingness (*egg* is a name for zero and Shakespeare uses *egg* in several plays to denote an object without value) and cannibalism (the eating of the egg) come together when the Fool tells Lear: 'Nuncle, give me an egg, and I'll give thee two crowns.' 'What two crowns shall they be?' asks Lear.

> *Why, after I have cut the egg i' th' middle and eat up the meat, the two crowns of the egg. When thou clovest thy crown i' the middle, and gav'st away both parts, thou bor'st thine ass on thy back o'er the dirt: thou hadst little wit in thy bald crown when thou gav'st thy golden one away.*
>
> (I.4.165–71)

Near the end of the play Edgar tells Gloucester of his fall: 'Thou'dst shiver'd like an egg; but thou dost breathe ...' (IV.6.51). These references to eggs also make us think of the 'germens' (III.2.8).

Albany's speeches to Goneril (IV.2.31–50) repeat many of these metaphors and images:

> *I fear your disposition:*
> *That nature, which contemns it origin,*
> *Cannot be border'd certain in itself;*
> *She that herself will sliver and disbranch*
> *From her material sap, perforce must wither*
> *And come to deadly use.*

Here we have a problem of boundaries and identity, words for cracking and breaking, and the image of the family tree. Albany continues:

> *Tigers, not daughters, what have you perform'd?*
> *A father, and a gracious aged man,*
> *Whose reverence even the head-lugg'd bear would lick,*
> *Most barbarous, most degenerate! have you madded.*
> *Could my good brother suffer you to do it?*
> *A man, a prince, by him so benefited!*
> *If that the heavens do not their visible spirits*
> *Send quickly down to tame these vile offences,*
> *It will come,*
> *Humanity must perforce prey on itself,*
> *Like monsters of the deep.*

A bear has appeared before in Lear's speech (III.4.8–11) but in this case it is necessary to know the old belief that baby bears were born as formless lumps and that the mother licked her cubs into shape—hence the origin of the idiom. *Head-lugg'd* means pulled by the head. Albany says that even a bear in a bad temper, because of being tugged by its ear or led by pulling on its head, would be kinder than Goneril and Regan. This, like *Tigers*, is another image of their ferocity. Thus Shakespeare is thinking of parents and their offspring in relation to savage behaviour, and of identity and character in terms of shape and it leads him to the monstrous notion of the children devouring the parents. Albany, like Gloucester when he talks of things coming apart early in the play (I.2.107–20), is generalising about all human life from the actions of two or three persons. Again Shakespeare is inviting us to consider the symbolic meaning of his play. Only by studying Shakespeare's metaphors can we know his thoughts. Metaphor is Shakespeare's way of bringing the whole accumulated power of the play to bear in almost every speech.

Part 4

Hints for study

THE MAIN THING is to know the play well and this, because of the difficulty, complexity and profundity of Shakespeare, can only be achieved by painstaking re-reading. *King Lear* needs to be read carefully at least three or four times in order that the reader can begin to have a grasp of the play as a whole, but there is, of course, no limit to the number of times that Shakespeare's greatest plays can be read with profit. Each time we discover something new. As we grow older, our understanding deepens as we keep bringing new experience to the text.

Two very useful exercises to accompany re-reading are to learn a number of the major speeches by heart and to translate the most crucial speeches or scenes into modern English, trying to find a modern equivalent for each of Shakespeare's words, without leaving out any of his meanings or connotations. The following are good speeches to memorise from *King Lear*:

(1) EDMUND: 'Thou, Nature, art my goddess ...' (I.2.1–22)
(2) LEAR: 'O! reason not the need ...' (II.4.266–88)
(3) LEAR AND THE FOOL: 'Blow winds ...' (III.2.1–36)
(4) ALBANY: 'O Goneril! ...' (IV.2.31–50)
(5) EDGAR: 'Come on sir ...' (IV.6.11–24)
(6) LEAR: 'What! art mad? ...' (IV.6.151-75)
(7) LEAR: 'No, no, no no! ...' (V.3.8–26)

There is probably no better way of coming to grips with the plot of *King Lear* (or any Shakespeare play) than to make an outline such as the one on page 41: read each scene and write a summary of what transpires (whether it is action that takes place between characters or an event that happens within a character) in one or two short sentences. Next mark every crisis or turning point and the moments of greatest intensity, and then consider how Shakespeare builds up to them, what consequences he derives from them, and how generally he keeps the story moving. Study how many stories are being told in the play and the relations between the main story and the subplot or subplots.

To have a clear sense of the personality of any major character, go through the play reading only the speeches of that character. The essential question to ask is: does the character change? and, if so, how and why? This can sometimes be seen more clearly by making two lists: the ways in which the character changes and the things about the character that remain constant throughout the play.

It is impossible to follow the metaphors and images of the play without taking extensive notes. Every time a metaphor or an image is repeated, or an important topic is mentioned, note the act, scene and line numbers. Arrange the notes by subject. For *King Lear* the notes ought to include all the references to: nature, justice, the gods or fate, ingratitude, animals, monsters, dogs, cracking or breaking or loss of shape, tears, clothing and the tortured movement of the human body. Having made the notes, think about the relations between the major topics of the play and the metaphors and images that are repeated most often. Try to establish both *what* Shakespeare is saying and *how* he is saying it. For example, in *King Lear* Shakespeare is very concerned with the difference between appearance and reality. This is expressed in many different ways: in the contrast of flattery and telling the truth, in the opposition of Lear's foolishness to the Fool's wisdom and in the metaphors of clothing, where the sumptuous exteriors of the rich are contrasted with the naked, often disagreeable, truths of human nature.

The most difficult thing in studying Shakespeare is to describe how Shakespeare uses language. There has been remarkably little written about Shakespeare's style, especially in view of the enormous number of books about Shakespeare. The following works are the ones that provide the most help with this difficulty and with the problem of understanding exactly what Shakespeare's words mean:

(1) The best edition in which to read Shakespeare is the New Arden Shakespeare. The texts are eclectic and the criticism in the introductions is often weak, but, most important, the editors gloss more individual words and construe more speeches than any other edition. Consequently they provide the most support for the ordinary reader. There is, in addition, a generous selection of Shakespeare's sources in the appendices. If this edition is not available, you could use the New Variorum Shakespeare, The New Penguin Shakespeare or the old Arden Shakespeare (in that order).

(2) C.T. ONIONS: *A Shakespeare Glossary*, Oxford University Press, Oxford, second edition revised, 1969, provides definitions of the words and the senses of words that have gone out of use since Shakespeare's time or offer special problems. An especially valuable book for anyone who does not have an annotated Shakespeare.

(3) A concordance is needed in order to find out how often Shakespeare has used a given word and in what contexts. The best is probably Marvin Spevack's *A Complete and Systematic Concordance to the Works of Shakespeare*, 6 volumes, Olms Hildesheim, 1968–70, but John Bartlett's one-volume *A New and Complete Concordance* London, 1894; Macmillan, London, 1960, will do just as well.

(4) E.A. ABBOTT: *A Shakespearean Grammar*, London, 1869; Dover, New York, 1966 is the standard work on this subject. He discusses such topics as Shakespeare's prepositions, verbs, relative constructions, compound words and prosody. This is an excellent book for elucidating syntactical difficulties and for information about the grammatical norms of Shakespeare's time.

(5) ERIC PARTRIDGE: *Shakespeare's Bawdy*, London, second edition, 1968; Dutton, New York, 1969, glosses the bawdy words in Shakespeare which are ignored or passed over by most editors.

(6) CAROLINE SPURGEON: *Shakespeare's Imagery*, Beacon, Boston, 1961, attempts to count all Shakespeare's images. Her results are somewhat problematical, because it is difficult to say in Shakespeare where one image ends and another begins, and because in some cases the nature of the image depends on the textual reading adopted. She also discusses Shakespeare's view of the world basing this examination on his images, and identifies what she believes are the most significant images in many of his plays. Edward Armstrong's *Shakespeare's Imagination*, University of Nebraska Press, Lincoln, 1965, is the best book on Shakespeare's style. He examines the clusters of images that are repeated in Shakespeare and proceeds to a study of Shakespeare's processes of association.

The following are some things to keep in mind when writing essays and examination papers:

☐ Read the directions very carefully three or four times so as to be certain to answer the right number of questions and to allow the right amount of time for each question.

☐ Reply directly to the question asked. (If the wording is ambiguous, it is proper to discuss the various ways in which it might be understood and to indicate the way in which you understand it in the first paragraph of your answer.)

☐ Outline your answer before starting to write. If writing an examination, note down any key passages or phrases from the text that you happen to remember before starting as it is easy to forget these in the course of writing.

☐ Be careful to write so that your answer is easy to read. It makes no difference how good it is if it is illegible.

☐ For every generalisation, give a particular example.

☐ Usually it is a good idea to make several different points rather than concentrating on a single one.

☐ Be specific.

☐ For most people the prerequisite to writing good essays is extensive revision. Be ready to discard whole paragraphs and if necessary completely re-write the entire essay.

☐ Be as simple, clear and direct as you can.
After finishing, check to be sure that what you have put down on paper is exactly what you were thinking. Very often we write something other than what we mean.

☐ Re-read what you have written before handing it in. Correct the spelling and punctuation, cross out unnecessary words, improve the phrasing if possible and add other examples if any important ones have suddenly occurred to you. It is occasionally necessary to recopy sections of an examination so that the whole answer is easy to read.

☐ Do not leave an examination early. Use all the time allowed.

Specimen questions

(1) What are the major turning points in *King Lear* and how are they related?

(2) What is the tragedy of *King Lear*?

(3) Analyse the character of King Lear.

(4) Compare Lear and Gloucester.

(5) What is the function of the Fool in *King Lear*?

(6) Discuss the relations between parents and children in *King Lear*.

(7) Is Cordelia's death justified?

(8) What does Edmund mean when he says: 'Thou, Nature, art my goddess' (I.2.1) and how is nature seen in *King Lear*?

(9) How does Shakespeare show us King Lear's madness?

(10) Write an interesting essay on the animal imagery in *King Lear*.

(11) What happens when Lear encounters Edgar disguised as 'poor Tom' (III.4) and what is the significance of this scene in the play as a whole?

(12) Identify the speaker and the occasion of each of the following speeches and discuss the relevance of what is said to the play as a whole:

(a) 'Thou art a soul in bliss; but I am bound / Upon a wheel of fire, that mine own tears / Do scald like molten lead.'

(b) 'Ripeness is all.'

(c) 'O! how this mother swells up towards my heart; / *Hysterica passio*! down, thou climbing sorrow! / Thy element's below.'

(13) 'A man's character is his fate.' To what extent is this statement true in *King Lear*?

Specimen answers

(1) What idea of justice is presented in *King Lear*?

Throughout *King Lear*, Shakespeare invites the spectator to consider the justice of each character's behaviour, but there are three scenes in which justice—and injustice—is handed down as in a court. These are: the division of the kingdom (I.1), the mock trial (III.6) and Edgar's fight to the death with Edmund (V.3).

The division of the kingdom is the act that sets the whole tragedy in motion. The scene is *at court*. The King is the judge. Goneril, Regan and Cordelia are the defendants. The first speeches of the play are on whether the proposed division is just: Kent asks whether Lear has not preferred one of the Dukes to the other; Gloucester replies that that may have been the case, but that now the shares drawn on the map are equal. To divide the kingdom is an irresponsible act. The rest of the play shows that justice will not be done in the kingdom as a whole if the King does not assume the responsibilities of power. Lear's foolishness, however, goes even further. He puts his daughters on trial as if to find out which one loves him the most, and, unjustly, makes the fate of the kingdom depend on their declarations of love. Lear shows himself to be a poor judge of character. He prefers the bad to the good when he rules against Cordelia and banishes Kent. The first scene is an image of justice gone wrong.

The mock trial takes place after Lear, the Fool, Edgar (disguised as Tom O'Bedlam) and Kent have taken shelter from the storm at Gloucester's castle. It, like the division of the kingdom, is a parody of justice. Lear decides to try his daughters again, but this time only Goneril and Regan. He uses legal language: 'I will arraign them straight' and calls Edgar 'most learned justicer'. The Fool and Edgar sit beside him as his bench of judges.

All three are bedraggled by the storm, Edgar smeared with mud and wrapped in a blanket. Two stools represent the two daughters. This is a pathetic image of justice: two madmen and a Fool. As rich clothing is often used in the play to stand for hypocrisy, their unkempt appearance promises honesty. The mock trial however, is inconclusive. This is part of its pathos. Nevertheless, Lear's resort to legal forms shows him attempting to re-establish order in his own mind. He is looking for justice rather than revenge, and trying to see beyond himself to the motives of others. He wants to discover if 'there is any cause in nature that makes these hard hearts?'

The final trial is the trial by combat of Edgar and Edmund in the concluding scene in which good destroys evil and justice is restored to the kingdom. This trial gets under way with all the ritual of a court of law: a herald reading the charge, the trumpet calls, and Albany acting virtually as referee. As a result Edmund confesses his crimes and tries unsuccessfully to make reparation for them.

These three trials reveal the difficulties and imperfections of human justice, but *King Lear* is about both human and divine justice. Shakespeare cannot consider whether men are just without asking if the world is just. Gloucester after he has been blinded challenges the justice of the Gods, who, he says, torment men as wanton boys kill flies for sport. When the mad Lear encounters the blind Gloucester, he challenges all man-made justice, because it is impossible to tell the judge from the thief, and because the rich buy justice. After he has defeated Edmund, Edgar declares that 'The Gods are just', but Lear weeping over the corpse of Cordelia calls the justice of life into question: 'Why should a dog, a horse, a rat, have life / And thou no breath at all?' Shakespeare explores the limits, complexity, and cost of human justice, and leaves us with our doubts about any other form of justice.

(2) **Explain how the following speech fits into the play and comment on Shakespeare's use of language:**

> Blow, winds, and crack your cheeks! rage! blow!
> You cataracts and hurricanoes, spout
> Till you have drench'd our steeples, drown'd the cocks!
> You sulph'rous and thought-executing fires,
> Vaunt-couriers of oak-cleaving thunderbolts,
> Singe my white head! And thou, all-shaking thunder,
> Strike flat the thick rotundity o' th' world!
> Crack Nature's moulds, all germens spill at once
> That makes ingrateful man!

This is the first speech by Lear in his madness. Near the end of Act II, Scene 4, after Goneril and Regan have both refused him, Lear declares that his heart will break into a hundred thousand pieces before he will weep. He tells the Fool: 'I shall go mad.' Here, at the beginning of Act III, Scene 2, his prophecy is fulfilled, except that it is not his heart but his mind that has broken.

The speech has two functions: to create the illusion of the external storm on the stage (in a theatre that had virtually no scenery or other effects) and to show us the internal storm of Lear's feelings.

The language is violent and emphatic. Lear's feelings, after being so long repресssed, burst forth in this storm of words. The speech is formed of a series of imperatives: 'blow', 'crack', 'rage', 'blow', 'spout', 'singe', 'strike', 'crack', 'spill'. Each sentence is an order for destruction that ends with an exclamation mark. Having submitted to his daughters, Lear now acts the king again. Having failed to command his daughters and his kingdom, he tries to command the elements. That he calls the thunderbolts 'vaunt-couriers' suggests that he imagines himself still surrounded by servants. The world has disobeyed him so, like a child, he wills the destruction of the whole world. His imperatives also represent a desperate attempt to order his inner world.

'Blow, winds, and crack your cheeks' personifies the winds, and provides a self-image of Lear: he is in the midst of the storm cracking his cheeks with rage. 'Sulph'rous' fires suggest hell-fire: punishment for sin and the welling-up of unpleasant forces from the under-world of the unconscious. Earlier, Lear thinks of his sorrows as coming from below, when, fighting off his feelings, he cries out: '*Hysterica passio!* down, thou climbing sorrow! Thy element's below.' Later, when he meets Gloucester, he imagines women's sexual passions as hellish and speaks of 'the sulphurous pit.' The association of sulphur with thunder and lightning in the storm scene gives us an image of heaven and hell together. Lear in this sentence turns his aggression against himself in directing the lightning to 'singe my white head'. He stands like an ancient and solitary oak cleft by a thunderbolt.

'Hurricanoes' is probably a word coined by Shakespeare and shows his gift for finding a special word for a special occasion. Similarly, 'thought-executing' which subordinates the lightning to Lear's will and makes the storm an image of his anger, is unusual and seems to have been created for this speech. It also suggests the speed of lightning: as rapid as thought. The intensity of Lear's feelings is expressed not only by the many violent imperatives, but also by the several compound words: 'thought-executing', 'vaunt-couriers', 'oak-cleaving' and 'all-shaking', four in three successive lines.

At the end of this speech, Lear calls upon the storm to destroy the moulds and germens or seeds from which man is created. This is like the curse that he pronounces on Goneril to prevent her from having children. Lear finds his daughters' ingratitude so unbearable that he thinks of all men as 'ingrateful' and seeks to destroy them all.

(3) Where does the phrase 'unaccommodated man' occur in *King Lear* and what is its significance?

The phrase occurs in Act III. Kent and the Fool have persuaded Lear to come in out of the storm. They take shelter in a hovel where they find Edgar disguised as a mad beggar, his body smeared with mud and wearing only a blanket. Thus, Lear, who is mad, is brought face to face with Edgar who is pretending to be mad; just as later, Lear, who has not seen the world as it is, confronts Gloucester, who is blind. When Lear looks at Edgar, he immediately sees himself: 'Didst thou give all to thy daughters?/And art thou come to this?'

Lear talks easily to Edgar, and, at one point, he tells him that he would be better dead than to be out in the storm with his 'uncover'd body'. Lear then thinks of Edgar as representing all mankind. 'Is man no more than this?' he asks. Most animals have a hide to protect them, the sheep has wool, but man has nothing. Edgar is 'the thing itself; unaccommodated man', no more than 'a poor, bare, forked animal'. 'Unaccommodated' means having none of the things that men have made for themselves in order to survive in the world, such as clothing and weapons. Edgar, as Lear sees him, is a man without culture, no more than another animal, an image of the essential poverty of human nature.

The language recalls Lear's argument with Goneril and Regan over the size of his retinue. There Lear argues that even the basest beggars have something superfluous to their minimum needs, and that if they do not, then 'Man's life is as cheap as beast's'. Here Edgar appears as a living example of Lear's argument: he is one of the basest beggars; he barely has what he needs to live; his life is that of a beast.

Lear in this scene is himself virtually another 'unaccommodated man'. He has been rejected by his family and turned out into the storm. He has been wandering on the barren heath in weather that Kent describes as 'too rough / For nature to endure'. He has neither home nor hearth to which to go. He has lost his mind and has nothing else to lose. Therefore, it is no surprise that he recognises himself in Edgar. His response to Edgar's condition is to try to take off his clothes. This is an attempt by Lear to discover his own essential self, to find the truth of his own human nature. It is also an attempt to be like Edgar, an act of brotherhood.

Part 5

Suggestions for further reading

The text

The most helpful edition in which to read the play is:
MUIR, KENNETH (ED.): *King Lear*, (The Arden Shakespeare) Methuen, London, 1959.
This is the edition used in the compilation of these Notes.

Other useful editions are:
HOUGHTON, R. E. C. (ED.): *King Lear*, (The New Clarendon Shakespeare) Clarendon Press, Oxford, 1978.
HUNTER, G. K. (ED.): *King Lear*, (The New Penguin Shakespeare) Penguin Books, Harmondsworth, 1972.

Other writings of Shakespeare

The best one-volume edition of Shakespeare is:
ALEXANDER, PETER (ED.): *The Complete Works*, Collins, London, 1951; paperback HarperCollins, Glasgow, 1994.

Also recommended is:
WELLS, STANLEY and TAYLOR, GARY (EDS): *The Complete Works*, Clarendon Press, Oxford, 1986. The compact edition followed in 1988.

General reading

Biography and background
The best one-volume introduction to Shakespeare's life and work is G. E. Bentley's short and lucid *Shakespeare, A Biographical Handbook*, Yale University Press, New Haven, 1961. The most detailed biography is S. Schoenbaum, *William Shakespeare, A Documentary Life*, Oxford University Press, Oxford, 1975. E. K. Chambers's *William Shakespeare*, two volumes, Clarendon Press, Oxford, 1930, reprinted 1988, remains an authoritative examination of Shakespeare's life and of the problems presented by the texts of his works. The second volume is useful because it contains complete translations of the major documents of Shakespeare's life and a compendium of all the earliest references to Shakespeare.

Shakespeare's England, two volumes, Oxford University Press, 1916, edited by Sidney Lee and C. T. Onions, is a good place to look for information about Shakespeare's world. A useful general reference book, alphabetically arranged, is Peter Bayley's *An A·B·C of Shakespeare*, (Longman York Handbooks) Longman, Harlow, 1985.

Criticism
The most useful books to help with the reading of individual passages and an understanding of Shakespeare's style are listed above (See pp. 63–4). Reading other plays by Shakespeare will contribute more to an understanding of King Lear than reading all the criticism written about the play. Shakespeare's poems also offer many clues to how he thinks.

Harley Granville-Barker's 'King Lear' in his *Prefaces to Shakespeare*, II, London, 1930; Batsford, London, 1963, reissued 1982, is especially recommended because it is a discussion of the problems of staging and acting the play by perhaps the most famous modern director of Shakespeare. There is an interesting essay by G. Wilson Knight on 'The Lear Universe' in his *The Wheel of Fire*, Methuen, London, 1959. *Shakespeare*, edited by Stanley Wells, Oxford University Press, Oxford, 1973; new edition, Clarendon Press, Oxford, 1990, is a bibliographical guide to Shakespeare and contains a chapter by Kenneth Muir reviewing the criticism of *King Lear*.

The following titles may also be of interest:
BLOOM, HAROLD (ED.): *King Lear*, (Modern Critical Interpretations) Chelsea House, New York and London, 1987.
BOOTH, STEPHEN (ED.): *King Lear, Macbeth: Indefinition and Tragedy*, Yale University Press, New Haven, 1983.
COOKSON, LINDA and LOUGHREY, BRYAN (EDS): *Critical Essays on King Lear*, (Longman Literature Guides) Longman, Harlow, 1988.
LERNER, LAWRENCE (ED.): *Shakespeare's Tragedies: An Anthology of Modern Criticism*, Penguin Books, Harmondsworth, 1963.
MUIR, KENNETH (ED.): *King Lear: Critical Essays*, Garland, New York and London, 1984.
MUIR, KENNETH (ED.): *King Lear: A Critical Study*, Penguin Books, Harmondsworth, 1986.
STEWART, J. I. M.: *Character and Motive in Shakespeare*, Longman, London, 1949; reissued 1965.

Essays on *King Lear* may be found in the following collections:
BRADLEY, A. C.: *Shakespearean Tragedy*, third edition by J. R. Brown, Macmillan, Basingstoke, 1982.
MUIR, EDWIN: *Essays on Literature and Society*. Hogarth Press, London, 1949.
ORWELL, GEORGE: 'Lear, Tolstoy and the Fool' in *Shooting an Elephant and Other Essays*, Secker, London, 1950.

The author of these notes

ROBERT M. REHDER is a poet whose work has appeared in a number of periodicals and anthologies. His contributions to Persian studies include 'The Unity of the Ghazals of Hafiz' (*Der Islam*, 1974), 'The Style of Jalal al-din Rumi' (*The Scholar and the Saint*, 1975) and translations in the Penguin *Anthology of Islamic Literature*, 1964. He is in the process of translating Hafiz for the Penguin Classics. He has written on Mallarmé and on Hardy, and is working on a book about *Wordsworth and the Beginnings of Modern Poetry*. He is a Senior Lecturer in English Studies in the University of Stirling.